Introduction to
Canadian Power and Sail Squadrons

Your decision to take this course exposes you to boating knowledge, techniques and skills, and the promise of new friends.

Our courses are intended to acquaint you with many important aspects of boat usage, and provide introduction to more detailed courses. The topics apply to pleasure craft of any size.

The following information introduces you with our Organization and its activities.

The Boating Course

Part I – Boating Basics

All operators of motorized pleasure craft are required to show proof of operator competency. All you need to know for the Transport Canada test is presented in an easy to read format that is both informative and entertaining. You can be confident that this study guide meets all the standards established by Transport Canada's Office of Boating Safety.

As an extra benefit, if you pass the test offered by Canadian Power and Sail Squadrons, your Card is recognized by BOTH Transport Canada and The National Association of State Boating Law Administrators (USA). You may contact Canadian Power and Sail Squadrons to locate a testing facility in your area.

Part II – Boating Essentials

Enjoyment and safety on the water require knowledge. Boating Essentials will take you to the next level in your boating education. Technology has changed the way we navigate. However, in order to use a GPS/chartplotter effectively, you should understand the use of paper charts and coastal navigation. The topics covered in this course; magnetic compass, global positioning and charts, navigation, conning, plotting, digital charting, anchoring, lines and ropes

will increase your boating knowledge and make your adventures on the water safe and enjoyable.

CPS-ECP Membership

After you have successfully completed the Boating course and examination you will receive a complimentary, one year regular membership in CPS-ECP. CPS-ECP is a nationwide group of boaters whose mandate is to teach and increase your knowledge of all phases of seamanship and navigation for both power and sail. The knowledge you gain will make your boating experiences both safe and more enjoyable.

You are encouraged to participate in social events which are an important part of membership in CPS-ECP where you will meet men and women with interests similar to your own.

Member

A Member of CPS-ECP is an individual who is at least 19 years of age and who:

a) has successfully completed a course prescribed** by the Board of Directors; or

b) holds a valid Pleasure Craft Operator Certificate (PCOC)

** PRESCRIBED COURSE is any CPS-ECP course or equivalent as per the Competency Equivalence Table.

Associate

An Associate is an individual who is less than nineteen (19) years of age but meets all of the other requirements of becoming a Member, and has applied to be an Associate. Any Associate who reaches age nineteen (19) may apply to become a Member. Please note: while being an Associate means having all of the privileges of membership, except for voting rights and signing authority, an Associate is not a member of CPS-ECP.

There are many opportunities in CPS-ECP for rewarding experiences. Boat ownership is not a requirement.

Module 1

Section 1.0

Section 2.0

Section 3.0

Section 4.0

Section 5.0

Section 6.0

Section 7.0

Module 2

Section 1.0

Section 2.0

Section 3.0

Section 4.0

Section 7.0

Appendices

Note: Penalties quoted in this manual are mandated by the Radiocommunications Act and Regulations. See Appendix 3—Contraventions Act.

Note: Except for Appendix 3, the material in the appendices is not examinable.

Maritime
Radio Course
Student's Notes

Section 1

module 1

1.0: Maritime mobile service

The Maritime Mobile Service encompasses Marine radiotelephone communications received and transmitted by ship stations on the VHF, MF and HF bands. Generally, the only land-based stations authorized to use this service are Canadian Coast Guard Radio Stations and Search and Rescue Facilities. In special cases, marinas, bridge and lock operators, airports in proximity to navigable waters and others having a valid reason to use marine radio from shore may be issued licences that permit operation on one or more specific channels, but usually not including VHF Channel 16 nor MF 2182kHz, which are the International Distress and Calling frequencies.

The VHF band provides fairly short range communications, typically of 20 nautical miles or so, depending on antenna height and terrain. Most pleasure boaters will only have a VHF radio. The MF and HF bands provide a much longer range communications, as far as a few thousand miles, depending on conditions. MF/HF equipment will normally only be found on vessels engaged in ocean voyages, although HF is used in the Arctic.

Location of radio (ship station)
The onboard radio should be located so as to:
(a) be secure and accessible
(b) enable the monitoring of distress and safety frequencies;
(c) protect it from the harmful effects of water and other adverse environmental conditions.

1.1 Regulations

1.1.1 Restricted Operator's Certificate (Maritime)

All persons operating a radio in Canadian waters must comply with regulations of their own country of origin. The certificate required by recreational marine operators based in Canada is the Restricted Operator's Certificate (Radiocommunication Regulations Part V). It is valid for the lifetime of the holder.

Any person who operates a radio in the Marine Bands without the appropriate certificate or authorization is liable for a conviction or a fine. See Appendix 3— Contraventions Act.

What is "operating a radio"? **Industry Canada's Legal Services has determined that the act of turning on a marine band radio is "operating".**

Upon successful completion of this course and examination, you will receive a Restricted Operator Certificate (Maritime), also known as a ROC(M), with a Digital Selective Calling (DSC) Endorsement. This certificate will entitle you to operate VHF, MF and HF Marine Band radios on a voluntarily fitted vessel. This certificate is also required by persons operating shore stations such as marina attendants, lock and bridge operators.

Voluntarily Fitted Vessels
These vessels include:
(a) Pleasure craft,
(b) Fishing vessels under 8 metres in length,
(c) Naval vessels,
(d) Tug boats operating only in restricted waters.

Compulsorily Fitted Vessels
(Section 7 Ship Regulations 1999)
All commercial vessels including:
(a) Ocean going vessels,
(b) Passenger carrying vessels,
(c) A closed construction ship of more than 8 metres in length
(d) Coastal freighters,
(e) Ice breakers,
(f) Tow boats.

Note: Operators on compulsorily equipped vessels usually will require a ROC(MC) (Maritime Commercial)

1.1.2 Radio station licence

A Marine Band radio installed on a vessel becomes a mobile station. Vessels meeting the requirements for exemption as set out in Section 15.2 of the Radiocommunications Act (See Appendix 5 for the Exemption of Radio Apparatus on Board a Ship or Vessel) are exempt from requiring a station licence. They must be operating in Canadian waters, or the waters of countries having a reciprocal agreement with Canada. The vessel must be using the operating frequencies listed in RBR-2, (Regulation By Reference-2, Technical Requirements for the Operation of Mobile Stations in the Maritime Service) (see Appendix 1). If the vessel is going to travel to a country that does not have a reciprocal agreement, a licence will be required.

In special cases, radio station licences may also be issued to marinas, bridge and lock operators, airports in proximity to navigable waters and others having a valid reason to use marine radio from shore.

Synopsis: When a vessel or aircraft is in the sovereign territory of any foreign administration, the provisions of the ITU (International Telecommunication Union) apply, which requires that all stations be licensed unless there is a treaty between the administrations involved. Boaters are advised that when travelling in U.S.A. waters, a radio station licence and an operator's certificate to operate the radio are required to fully comply with international law.

Currently, a Canadian vessel does not require a station license when in International waters. However, a station License is required when travelling in the waters of other countries. This can change at any time.

A station licence, when required, will be issued only to equipment which meets Industry Canada, Spectrum Management, approval. A nine (9) digit number, which appears on a label affixed to the back of the radio, indicates this approval. Some manufactures post this 9 digit number on their website in lieu of labelling the radio. Only equipment approved by Industry Canada can meet the requirement for a licence or qualify for exemption of a licence. It should be noted that equipment purchased in the United States might not

have this approval number. Any devices such as radar which emit radio waves and are installed on a vessel, must be included in this licence, when a licence is required. If any devices are added or deleted, it must be noted on the issued licence. If a licence is required, then that licence is to be posted in a conspicuous location near the radio equipment.

The licence is renewable annually, for a fee.

A station licence will not be issued to any person under the age of sixteen (16) years.

Any person or corporation who establishes a radio station without a licence, if a licence is required, is liable, upon summary conviction. See Appendix 3— Contraventions Act.

Note: Radiocommunication Act—September 10, 1998 Section 10(3) For licensing, certification and radio operation offences, if committed or continued on more than one day, the person who committed the offence is liable to be convicted for a separate offence for each day on which the offence is committed or continued. Section 10(6) Prosecution for any offence may be commenced within, but not after, three (3) years after the day on which it arose. See Appendix 3—Contraventions Act.

The radio station licence specifies the call sign assigned to the station, the frequencies to be used for transmitting, the type of radio equipment authorized, and any special conditions under which the station shall be operated. With regard to the permitted frequencies, the licence refers the operator to Regulation by Reference (RBR-2) which lists available frequencies for all of Canada. An excerpt from RBR-2 is shown in Appendix 1.

The frequencies available in Marine Bands include medium and high frequencies (MF-HF). In these bands the Distress and Calling frequency is 2182 kHz.

The frequencies most likely to be used on your vessel are known as Very High Frequency (VHF), in which the distress and calling frequency is 156.8 MHz (Channel 16).

1.1.3 Authorities

Industry Canada—Spectrum Management (ICSM)

Industry Canada is the Federal Government department which sets out and controls the regulations and procedures established by the International Telecommunications Union, by passing them into Canadian law.

International Telecommunications Union (ITU)

The ITU is the world body, made up of member countries, which controls radio regulations and procedures world-wide. Canada is one of the member countries. Any amendments to the regulations, procedures and frequency allocations must be forwarded to the ITU by Industry Canada before any changes can come into effect.

Coast Guard Radio (CGR)

The Canadian Coast Guard maintains search and rescue services and is a major user of marine radiotelephone. All distress and calling frequencies, including MF 2182 kHz and VHF Channel 16, are monitored by this group, coast to coast. To exercise these functions, they maintain effective control over the marine frequencies. Among the services available are weather broadcasts, notices to mariners, ship movement, public telephone, and most importantly, emergency services.

Coast Guard Radio Stations are identified by their geographical names, followed by "... Coast Guard Radio". Example: Thunder Bay Coast Guard Radio.

International Maritime Organization (IMO)

The International Maritime Organization is a branch of the United Nations that is responsible (amongst other things) for radio communications and search and rescue vessels at sea. There are 169 countries that subscribe to the IMO. Many of our rules and regulations originated with the IMO.

Figure 1.1: A Coast Guard Radio Station

1.1.4 Radio station requirements

Log keeping

Each station on a compulsorily equipped vessel is required to maintain a *Radio Log*. It is not mandatory for voluntarily fitted vessels, but it is strongly recommended that they keep a log especially of all *emergency* traffic. This should be retained in its original form as it may subsequently be required in some form of legal proceedings. It is considered good practice to keep an accurate Radio Log, and to record all entries legibly, so that they are clearly understood.

Radio watchkeeping

Prior to February 1, 2005, ships which were required by law to be fitted with a radiotelephone had to keep a continuous watch when at sea, on the frequency MF 2182 kHz and/or Channel 16 (VHF), (or other frequency specifically designated in their licences), except when actually engaged in conducting communications on their working frequencies. The introduction of the requirement that compulsorily fitted vessels have DSC has resulted in the belief that such vessels no longer need to monitor Channel 16.

However, document 'VHF Radiotelephone Practises and Procedures Regulations' dated March 2010 states that large commercial vessels (over 500 GRT) on international voyages must begin radio watch on Channel 16 at least fifteen (15) minutes before they leave the dock or mooring and continue to do so until at anchor or moored. Other vessels should endeavour to keep watch on the frequency MF 2182 kHz and/or VHF Channel 16 when at sea, to ensure that Distress, Urgency or Safety traffic will be heard by as many stations as possible.

Both the IMO and the ITU have passed resolutions recommending the same thing. Radio Aids to Marine Navigation (2010), part 4 – Procedures states that "Where practicable, and having due regard for Vessel Traffic Services and Seaway Control requirements, a conscientious listening watch should be maintained on VHF Channel 16".

Radio silence periods

No vessel shall transmit on MF 2182 kHz during the mandated silence period, other than in *emergency* situations. The *radio silence period commences on the hour and on the half hour and extends for three (3) minutes*. Compulsorily fitted vessels with MF must maintain a radio watch during these periods.

Note: Vessels fitted with VHF are not required to maintain a listening watch during these radio silence periods.

1.1.5 Documents

Canadian ship stations voluntarily fitted with a Marine Band radio (most pleasure boats) must carry the following documents:
(1) Ship Station Licence (or a copy thereof), unless exempted by regulations (See Appendix 5),
(2) Radio Operator's Certificate(s), for the persons operating the radio,

and should carry the following publications:
(1) *Radio Aids to Marine Navigation (Pacific or Atlantic, as appropriate)* (current edition),
(2) Manufacturer's Operating Manuals for the radio equipment in use.

Note: The <u>vessel</u> must carry a licence, (*if not exempt*) and the <u>operator</u> (*not the vessel*), must carry an operator's certificate."

Figure 1.2: Required Documents

Inspection of radio apparatus

Spectrum Management Officers must be given assistance and may, at any reasonable time, inspect *any vessel* fitted with radio equipment. The Inspectors shall not be obstructed or resisted, nor shall a false or misleading statement be made to them.

Any person who is found guilty, upon summary conviction, of an offence regarding radio apparatus inspection, shall be liable to a fine.

Where an offence is committed or continued on more than one day, the person who committed the offence is liable to be convicted for a separate offence for each day on which the offence is committed or continued. (Limitation of three (3) years.) See Appendix 3— Contraventions Act.

1.1.6 Secrecy of communications

Certain radiocommunications are privileged. Persons who become acquainted with such privileged communications are bound to preserve the secrecy of correspondence. Marine radio transmissions are such communications.

No person shall divulge the contents of, or even the existence of correspondence transmitted, received or intercepted by a radio station, except to the addressee of the message or his/her accredited agent, or to the properly authorized officials of the Government of Canada or a competent legal tribunal, or an operator of a telecommunications system as is necessary for the furtherance of delivery of the communications.

The foregoing restrictions do not apply to messages of Distress, Urgency or Safety or to messages addressed to *All Stations* or to broadcast information.

Any person who violates the secrecy of correspondence is liable, on summary conviction, to a fine and / or imprisonment.

1.1.7 The international distress, safety and calling frequencies of MF 2182 kHz and 156.8 MHz (VHF) Channel 16

These frequencies are primarily used for Distress, Urgency and Safety calls. They may be used for initial contacts and replies with other stations to *establish communications*. Once communication has been established, a change to a working frequency (appropriate channel designated intership or ship-to-shore) *must* be made for the resumption of communications. Communications other than the above are *not permitted* on these frequencies.

Avoid *excessive calling* on these frequencies, and ensure silence periods are maintained on MF 2182 kHz. All ship stations equipped to transmit on either, or both, of these frequencies should maintain a listening watch on these frequencies to the greatest extent possible.

The digital selective calling frequencies for distress are 156.525 MHz (VHF) Channel 70 and 2187.5 kHz (MF).

USCG terminated watchkeeping on MF 2182 kHz and DSC 2187.5 kHz on August 1st, 2013. Additionally, marine information and weather broadcasts transmitted by USCG were also terminated on that date. The Canadian CG however, continues to monitor MF 2182 kHz, DSC 2187.5 kHz, provides broadcast services on 2 MHz, and has no plans to discontinue this service

N.B. Channel 70 may not be used for voice communications. DSC-equipped radios will not permit voice transmissions on this channel.

1.1.8 Propagation and use of VHF transmitter power switch

Many factors affect radio propagation (the spreading of radio waves), and the maximum communication ranges can vary. Vessels fitted with a VHF transmitter of 25 watts output (maximum power authorized), and an efficient antenna, can be expected to operate up to distances of approximately 20 nautical miles ship to ship. This range can be drastically limited by land masses. VHF communications are commonly known as *line-of-sight* because the radio waves in the VHF band travel in straight lines. Range can be considerably greater ship to shore. To establish contact with another station within a harbour, or in close proximity, the calling station should transmit on 1 watt, and increase the power to 25 watts only when no response has been made to the call using the proper procedures.

1.1.9 Radio Frequency (RF) Exposure

The Departments of Industry (Industry Canada) and Health (Health Canada) work together to ensure that the general public is protected from the potential harmful effects of RF fields. Health Canada establishes safe limits of exposure (i.e. Safety Code 6) and Industry Canada ensures that all wireless infrastructure and devices comply with these limits. Compliance is a requirement of the Department's equipment certification process.

Based on the current scientific evidence, Health Canada's position is that radiofrequency exposure levels within the limits specified in Safety Code 6 do not cause adverse health effects.

A component of the compliance process includes demonstrating compliance with Canadian radiofrequency (RF) exposure limits. Industry Canada's

RSS-102, Radio Frequency Exposure Compliance of Radiocomm-unication Apparatus (All Frequency Bands), sets out the requirements and measurement techniques used to evaluate RF exposure compliance of radiocomm-unication apparatus used within the vicinity of the human body. RSS-102 is available at: http://strategis.ic.gc.ca/epic/internet/insmtgst.nsf/en/sf01904e.html

Handheld

A typical handheld VHF marine transceiver has a helical (rubber duck) antenna and a maximum output power of five watts. These devices must be certified for use in Canada and approved devices contain a label with an Industry Canada certification number. All handheld products bearing an Industry Canada label meet the RF exposure requirements of RSS-102.

Additional information on handheld VHF-DSC transceivers may be found in Module 2.

Fixed Mount VHF Radios

In addition to hand held transceivers, a marine operator may have a permanently installed VHF Marine transceiver with an external antenna. These transceivers have power outputs of one and twenty-five watts. In these instances, the antenna should be installed in a location that ensures a safe separation between the user and antenna.

Manufacturers are responsible for providing proper instructions to the user of the radio device as well as any usage restrictions such as limiting exposure durations. The user manual will contain installation and operation instructions and outline any special usage conditions to ensure compliance with Canadian RF exposure limits. The user manual will also caution against inappropriate usage and provide instructions regarding minimum separation distances between users or bystanders.

1.1.10 MF/HF and Single Sideband (SSB)

Most of this manual is concerned with VHF radio which is the most popular form of maritime radio. VHF is used for short range communication, typically about 20 nm between stations. Communications between ships and Coast Guard shore stations may be

considerably more than just 20 nm because the shore stations use very high antennas.

Vessels traveling far offshore can use MF or HF radios. These radios often use Single Sideband (SSB) transmissions which is a very effective form of communication.

In general, pleasure craft use VHF almost exclusively in inland waters and coastal communications. HF/MF is used mostly for offshore communications. The ROC(M) certificate is valid for operators of all maritime radios.

Those interested in more information on MF/HF should see Appendix 12. The appendices are for general information and with the exception of Appendix 3, they are not examinable.

1.1.11 Antennas

You are allowed to install your own antenna(s), although most boaters prefer to have this done by a professional. In general, the higher a VHF antenna, the better the reception as VHF is line of sight transmission. MF/HF antennas should be out of reach of passengers. crew or animals as it is possible to receive a jolt or a burn if an antenna is touched while transmitting. A poor antenna connection or an improper transmission cable can seriously reduce both sending and receiving.

Appendix 13, Propagation and Antennas (non-examinable) contains some additional information regarding antennas.

1.2 Shading

Some parts of this manual are shaded. This indicates that the information may be of interest, but is not examinable.

1

module 1

Maritime
Radio Course
Student's Notes

Section 2

2.0 Procedures

2.1 Uses of marine radio

You *may* use your Marine radio for:
(a) Distress and Safety messages,
(b) Operational messages,
(c) Business messages.

You *may not* use your Marine radio for:
(a) False Distress,
(b) Profane or offensive language,
(c) Superfluous transmissions,
(d) Establishing a land-based station.

Marinas and other shore-based organizations having a legitimate reason to communicate with vessels may obtain a special station licence authorizing them to use a specific channel.

2.1.1 False distress

False distress signals are strictly prohibited.

Large penalties are provided for any person indulging in such irresponsible behaviour.

*Penalty**

Any person who knowingly transmits or causes to be transmitted, any false or fraudulent distress signal, call or message, or who, without lawful excuse, interferes with or obstructs any radio communication, is guilty of an offence and is liable, on summary conviction, to a penalty not exceeding five thousand dollars ($5,000) and costs, or to imprisonment for a term not exceeding twelve months, or to both. The maximum penalty for a corporation is $25,000.

2.1.2 Profane and offensive language

Profane and offensive language is also strictly prohibited.

*Penalty**

Any person who violates the regulations relative to unauthorized communications or profane language is liable, upon summary conviction, to a penalty not exceeding five thousand dollars ($5,000) and costs, or to imprisonment for a term not exceeding one year, or to both. The maximum penalty for a corporation is $25,000.

2.1.3 Interference/superfluous transmissions

All radio stations shall be installed and operated so as not to interfere with, or interrupt, the working of another station. Superfluous transmission includes any transmission which does not further the purposes of the permitted uses (excessive conversation). Interference includes any transmissions which are not part of a two-way communication such as:

(a) Child playing with the microphone,
(b) Casual noise picked up by an open microphone,
(c) Background music picked up during an otherwise legitimate transmission,
(d) Running with an open microphone.

In other words, you are required to keep your transmissions 'clean'.

Penalty

Any person who, without lawful excuse, interferes with or obstructs any radiocommunication is guilty of an offence. That person is liable, on summary conviction, to a fine. See Appendix 3—Contraventions Act.

The only situation in which you may interrupt, or interfere with, the normal working of another station is to transmit a higher priority message, such as a distress, urgency, or safety call.

* If the offense is committed on or continued on more than one day, a separate conviction may be made for each day. Therefore, if the offense occurs over a five day period the penalty could be $5,000 and/or 5 years in jail.

2.2 Radio operation

2.2.1 Speech transmission techniques

Speak all words plainly, and end each word clearly, to prevent words from running together. Avoid any tendency to shout, to accent syllables artificially, or to talk too rapidly. The following points should be kept in mind when using a Marine radio:

Speed

Keep the rate of speaking constant, neither too fast nor too slow. Remember that the operator receiving your message may have to write it down.

Rhythm

Preserve the rhythm of ordinary conversation. Avoid the introduction of unnecessary sounds such as "er" and "um" between words.

2.2.2 Word spelling

The words of the International Telecommunications Union's (ITU) phonetic alphabet should be learned thoroughly, so that whenever isolated letters or groups of letters are pronounced separately, or when communication is difficult, the phonetic alphabet can be easily and fluently used.

When it is necessary to spell out words, the following letter spelling table shall be used:

Letter to be Transmitted	Word to be used
A	ALPHA
B	BRAVO
C	CHARLIE
D	DELTA
E	ECHO
F	FOXTROT
G	GOLF
H	HOTEL
I	INDIA
J	JULIETT
K	KILO
L	LIMA
M	MIKE
N	NOVEMBER
O	OSCAR
P	PAPA
Q	QUEBEC
R	ROMEO
S	SIERRA
T	TANGO
U	UNIFORM
V	VICTOR
W	WHISKEY
X	X-RAY
Y	YANKEE
Z	ZULU

2.2.3 Numbers

Number to be Transmitted	Word to be used
0	ZERO
1	ONE
2	TWO
3	THREE
4	FOUR
5	FIVE
6	SIX
7	SEVEN
8	EIGHT
9	NINE
	DECIMAL
	THOUSAND

Example: Using the phonetic alphabet, the vessel *Seadog* would express its identification as:

Sierra Echo Alpha Delta Oscar Golf,

if asked to spell the vessel name while communication was difficult.

All numbers, except for whole thousands, should be transmitted by pronouncing each digit separately. Whole thousands should be transmitted by pronouncing each digit in the number of thousands, followed by the word "thousand".

Example:

75	becomes	*Seven five*
100	becomes	*One zero zero*
5800	becomes	*Five eight zero zero*
11000	becomes	*One one thousand*
68009	becomes	*Six eight zero zero nine*

Numbers containing a decimal point shall be transmitted as the above with the decimal point indicated by the word "decimal".

Example:

156.8	becomes	*One five six decimal eight*

Channel designation shall be transmitted with the spoken word, "Channel", and each digit pronounced separately.

Example:

Channel *16*	becomes	*Channel one six*
Channel *68*	becomes	*Channel six eight*

Monetary denominations, when transmitted with groups of digits, should be transmitted in the sequence in which they are written.

Example:

$17.25	becomes	*Dollars one seven decimal two five*
75¢	becomes	*seven five cents* (that is, use the cent symbol if you want cents. As written it would be *decimal seven five*)

2.3 Procedural words and phrases

While it is not practical to set down precise phraseology for all Marine radio procedures, the following words and phrases should be used where applicable. Words and phrases such as "OK", "Repeat", "Ten-four", "Over and Out", "Breaker Breaker", "Come in please", or slang expressions should not be used.

Word or Phrase	Meaning
Acknowledge	Let me know that you have received and understood this message.
Affirmative	Yes, or permission granted.
Break	To indicate the separation between portions of the message. (To be used where there is no clear distinction between text and other portions of the message).
Channel	Change to channel…before proceeding.
Confirm	My version is…Is that correct?
Correction	An error has been made in this transmission (message indicated). The correct version is…
Go ahead	Proceed with your message.
How do you read?	How well do you receive me?
I say again	Self-explanatory (use instead of "I repeat.")
Mayday	The spoken word for the distress communications.
Mayday Relay	The spoken words for the distress relay signal.
Negative	No, or that is not correct, or I do not agree.
Over	My transmission is ended, and I expect a response from you.
Out	Conversation is ended, and no response is expected.

Word or Phrase	Meaning
Pan Pan	The spoken words for urgency communications.
Prudonce	During long distress situations, communication can resume on a restricted basis. Communication is to be restricted to ship's business or messages of a higher priority.
Read back	Repeat all of this message back to me exactly as received after I have given over (do not use the word "repeat").
Roger	Message received and understood.
Roger number	I have received your message Number ...
Stand by	I must pause for a few seconds or a few minutes; please wait.
Say again	Self-explanatory (do not use the word "repeat").
Sécurité	The spoken word for the safety signal.
Seelonce	Indicates that silence has been imposed on the frequency due to a distress situation.
Seelonce Distress	The international expression to advise that a distress situation is in progress. This command comes from a vessel or coast station other than the station in distress.
Seelonce feenee	The international expression for a distress cancellation.
Seelonce Mayday	The international expression to inform an individual(s) that a distress situation is in progress. The command issued from the ship in distress.
Urgency ended	Expression for Urgency cancellation
That is correct	Self-explanatory.
Verify	Check coding, check text with originator, and send correct version.
Wilco	Instructions received, understood and will be complied with.

Word or Phrase	Meaning
Words twice	(a) As a request: Communication is difficult, please send each word twice. (b) As information: Since communication is difficult, I will send each word twice.

2.4 Time

The twenty-four hour clock system should be used in expressing time in the Maritime Mobile Services. While a vessel is in local waters, local time may be used (Pacific Standard Time, Eastern Standard Time, etc.). When vessels are engaged in international voyages, Co-ordinated Universal Time (UTC) previously known as Greenwich Mean Time (GMT) should be used. The letter Z is an accepted abbreviation for UTC.

However, where operations are conducted entirely within one time zone, local time may be used. Care should be taken to clearly indicate the time zone involved, for example 1335E (for Eastern Standard Time), 1035P (for Pacific Standard Time).

2.4.1 Examples of transmission

Examples of time using the twenty-four hour clock system:

12:45	A.M.	is expressed as 0045
12:00	(NOON)	is expressed as 1200
12:45	P.M.	is expressed as 1245
12:00	(MIDNIGHT)	is expressed as 2400 or 0000
1:30	A.M.	is expressed as 0130
1:45	P.M.	is expressed as 1345
8:30	P.M.	is expressed as 2030

Examples of transmission of time:

0045	transmitted as	zero zero four five
1345	transmitted as	one three four five

2.4.2 Transmission of date

Where the date, as well as the time of day, is required to be shown, a six(6) figure group should be used. The first two figures indicate the day of the month; the following four figures indicate the time. See Appendix 4 for Time Zone Comparison Tables.

Noon on the 16th day of the month (EST)	is expressed as	161200E
2:29 a.m. PST on the 14th day of the month	is expressed as	140229P
4:45 P.M. AST on the 21st day of the month	is expressed as	211645A

2.5 Call signs

A distinctive *call sign* is assigned to radio stations requiring licensing, for identification purposes. It should be used when initial contact is being established, and again when the communication is concluded. In the case of *Ship Stations,* the call sign should follow the name of the ship.

Example:
Seabird II CZ5837

Call signs are issued with the vessel's radio Station License. Most pleasure craft are voluntarily fitted and do not require a radio Station License while in Canadian waters. Remember, **Canadian vessels with a maritime radio MUST have a Canadian radio Station Licence when in US waters (as well as in the waters of most other countries)**. Do not confuse radio Station Licenses with operator's certificates. An ROC(M) is mandatory if you operate a maritime radio (see section 1.1.1).

Because a call sign or a vessel name must be used both at the beginning of a call or contact and when signing off, the question arises "what do I use for a call sign if I do not choose to obtain a radio license?" If you do not have an assigned call sign, you may use the name of your boat, your own name, or other name you choose to use.

You must use that call sign or other identifier when signing off. When a call is concluded, all participants are required to sign off.

Call signs are extremely important for identification purposes, as more than one vessel may have the same name; whereas only *a unique call sign* is assigned to each ship station, regardless of vessel name.

Should a vessel not have a name, it shall be identified by call sign only.

Vessels not requiring a call sign should use a distinct vessel name when in communications. It is also suggested that they have the vessel's registration/licence numbers posted handy to the radio, so that they can be used for positive identification.

2.6 Calling

Instructions given here in Module 1 apply to vessels that are not equipped with DSC (Digital Selective Calling). Recreational boaters with VHF — DSC radios are encouraged to use DSC when calling another vessel. This will reduce the congestion frequently experienced using channel 16 to establish contact, as well as avoiding interference with distress communications, etc. Module 2 of this manual covers DSC communications.

Before transmitting on the calling channel, every operator shall listen for a period long enough to be satisfied that harmful interference to transmissions already in progress, will not occur.

Avoid 'Reverse' Calling
Remember that the *identity* of the station being *called* is always spoken *first*, followed by *this is* and your own station's identity.

A station having a Distress, Urgency or Safety Message to transmit is entitled to interrupt transmissions of lower priority at any time.

2.6.1 Procedure

To establish communications with a *specific* station, the following procedure should be used:

1. *Switch* on radio,

2. *Select* channel,

3. *Adjust* squelch and volume, think of the squelch control as a gate. If the squelch control is turned fully clockwise, it closes the gate so much that no signals get through. If the squelch control is turned

fully counterclockwise, it opens the gate so wide that everything gets through—noise, weak signals and strong signals. To set the 'squelch gate' to the desired level, the squelch control is turned counter clockwise until noise (hash) is heard. Then the squelch control is turned back clockwise just until the noise stops. Now the squelch is set properly.

4. *Listen* (always listen twice as long as you think is necessary).

5. *Place* your call in the following manner:
   (a) Depress transmit switch on microphone,
   (b) Call the station you wish to contact (not more than three times),
   (c) Say *This is,*
   (d) Say your station's name (not more than three times), on channel ...
   (e) Say *Over,*
   (f) Release the transmit switch,
   (g) Listen for an answer. If no response is received after two calls, wait at least three minutes or longer before calling again.

6. If a *response* is made to your call, it should take the following form:
   (a) Your station name (not more than three times),
   (b) *This is,*
   (c) The name of the replying station, (not more than three times), Switch to (name the working channel).
   (d) *Over.*

7. If the above call was made on a distress and calling frequency, a change to a *working* frequency must follow.

8. From this point on, normal traffic may be carried on.

9. When traffic is completed, *both* stations must sign off, using their respective names and call signs.

10. Both stations should then return to the distress/ calling frequency and maintain radio watch.

Balanced calling should be maintained. When calling another station's name *three times,* identify your

station's name *three times;* if calling another station's name *twice,* identify your station's name *twice,* and if calling the station *once,* identify your station *once.*

The above is the proper procedure to follow in establishing communications. This logical sequence is the key to all good calling. Many different types of calls will be appropriate from time to time, and each follows the same logical sequence. The following are examples of proper procedure.

2.6.2 Single station call (vessel calling another vessel, using Channel 16 to establish contact)

Note: The station name may be said once or, if communication conditions are difficult, not more than three times.

In the following example calls, West Coast users should substitute 'Channel 68' for 'Channel 71', as Channel 71 is used by the Vessel Traffic Service on the West Coast.

Call:
　　EAGLE
　　This is
　　SNOWGOOSE
　　OVER

Reply:
　　SNOWGOOSE
　　This is
　　EAGLE
　　Go to Channel 71
　　OVER

Response:
　　EAGLE
　　This is **SNOWGOOSE**
　　ROGER 71
　　OUT

Establishing Contact on Channel 71:
> **SNOWGOOSE**
> *This is*
> **EAGLE**
> **OVER**

Response:
> **EAGLE**
> *This is*
> **SNOWGOOSE**
> (message)

You need not use Channel 71 (or 68), you may choose any intership Channel that is useable in your area.

2.6.2.1 Signing off

When the communication is finished both stations must sign off using their call sign.

Eagle signs off:
> **Eagle OUT**

Snowgoose signs off:
> **Snowgoose OUT**

Having signed off (unless another call is being made) the stations should return to listening out on Channel 16.

Calling on Channel 16 (VHF) to make contact with another station is permitted. However, to help reduce congestion on Channel 16 due to calling during periods of heavy traffic (summer weekends, etc.), it is suggested that stations wishing to communicate with other specific stations make contact on a *working channel,* at a predetermined time. A listening watch on Channel 16 must still be maintained before and after communicating on the working channel.

2.6.3 Single station call (vessel calling a Coast Guard radio station)

Call: **HALIFAX COAST GUARD RADIO**
> *This is*
> **MALLARD**
> *on Channel 26*
> **OVER**

Expected Response:
> **MALLARD**
> *This is*
> **HALIFAX COAST GUARD RADIO**
> *Go Ahead*
> **OVER**

In areas where radio traffic is heavy, it is good operational procedure to *initially* try to make contact with the Coast Guard Radio Station on one of their *working channels*. In areas where radio traffic is moderate, Channel 16 may be used.

When calling a Coast Guard radio station, always state the Channel on which you are calling as the Coast Guard radio operator will be monitoring several channels.

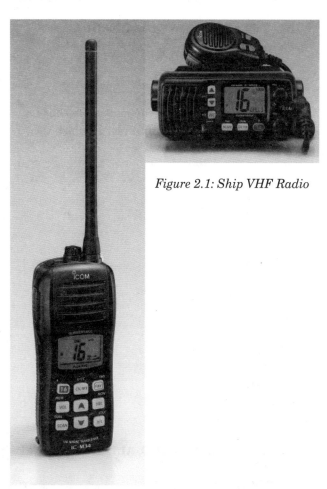

Figure 2.1: Ship VHF Radio

Figure 2.2: Hand-held VHF Radio

2.6.4 General call
(vessel calling "All Stations")

To establish contact with any station within range, or in a given area, call as follows:

**ALL STATIONS ALL STATIONS
ALL STATIONS**
This is
EMU EMU EMU
*Any vessel with weather information,
Thunder Cape area*
Switch to Channel 71
OUT

2.6.5 Multiple station call
(vessel calling more than one vessel)

BLUESEAS, WINDWARD, ALTAIR
This is
CONDOR II,
OVER

As a general rule, operators replying to a *multiple* station call should answer in the order in which they have been called.

CONDOR
This is
BLUESEAS
OVER

CONDOR
This is
WINDWARD
OVER

CONDOR
This is
ALTAIR
OVER

Response:
BLUESEAS, WINDWARD, ALTAIR
This is
CONDOR
Switch to Channel 71
OUT

Note: After establishing contact on the working channel, messages may be exchanged.

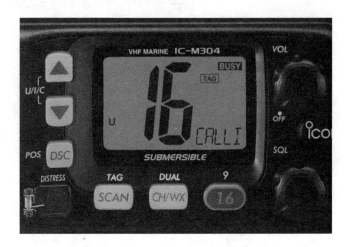

Figure 2.3: General call on Channel 16

2.6.6 Replying to calls
when information is missing

When you hear a call, but are uncertain the call is intended for your station, do not reply until the call is repeated and understood.

When your station is called but the identity of the calling station is uncertain, you should reply immediately, using the words:

STATION CALLING
This is
(your station's identification)
SAY AGAIN
OVER

2.7 Choice of frequencies

Frequency assignment varies according to regions in Canada:
(a) Each *Station Licence* (if required) refers the operator to RBR-2, schedule 1, for the list of authorized frequencies and their assigned use.
(b) Information for other regions can be obtained from a Regional or District office of Industry Canada— Spectrum Management.

(c) The *Radio Aids to Marine Navigation* publication for each region should also be consulted. (See Appendix 9)

(d) RBR-2 Schedule 1, which lists VHF channel assignments, is included in this manual as Appendix 1.

2.7.1 Channel groups

Modern marine VHF radios permit the user to select one of three channel groups or modes: *Canada, United States.* or *International.* The *Canada, United States.* and *International* channel groups are factory-programmed by the manufacturer in accordance with Industry Canada (Canada), FCC (U.S.A.) and International regulations, respectively. Marine VHF radios purchased in North America are generally supplied by the manufacturer with the U.S.A. channel group selected by default. Switching from one channel group to another is typically accomplished using a U/I/C (U.S.A./International/Canada) control or combination of controls on the radio. The user should consult the instruction manual provided by the manufacturer for details. Older radios may only have

U.S. and International modes. In that case, the radio should be left in the U.S. mode except when using a Canadian duplex channel that would be simplex in the U.S. mode.

In order to ensure compliance with the rules and regulations of the country in whose waters you are boating, it is important that you select the channel group appropriate for your area of operation. For example, the Canada channel group consists of those channels designated by Industry Canada in Schedule 1 of RBR-2. Since these are the only channels on which one may legally operate in Canadian waters, any vessel operating its marine VHF radio in Canadian waters should have the Canada channel group selected. Both the U.S.A. and International channel groups contain some channels that are not authorized by Industry Canada for use by mobile stations in the maritime service. Similarly, when boating in U.S. waters, the U.S.A. channel group should be selected in order to comply with FCC regulations.

The selection of the appropriate channel group for the area of operation also serves to facilitate

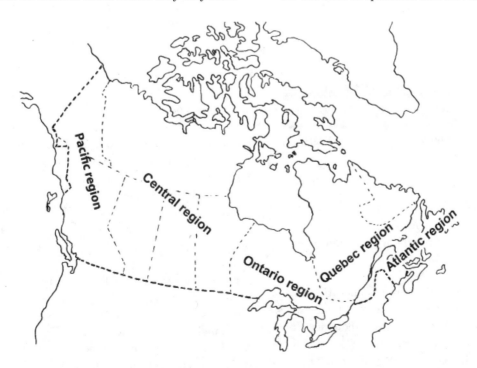

Figure 2.4: Industry Canada regions

communication with other vessels and authorized coast stations in the area. For example, if you were directed by CCG to go to channel 62A and your radio was set to other than the Canada channel group, channel 62A would not be available to you.

The table in Appendix 2 identifies the channels in each of the three channel groups at this time. The table indicates the international channel designators currently found in any publication of marine VHF channels from an official source. It should be noted that some variations in the channels may be programmed into each group. Various displays may be encountered depending on the manufacturer of the radio and its date of manufacture.

2.7.2 Channel types and designations

A marine VHF radio channel may be a *simplex* channel or a *duplex* channel.

A simplex channel is a channel on which a radio transmits and receives on the same frequency. If two stations attempt to transmit simultaneously, the frequency will be jammed for all users.

For example, Channel 16 is a simplex channel as indicated in Table 2.1.

Channel	Type	Vessel's Transmit Frequency (MHz)	Vessel's Receive Frequency (MHZ)
16	simplex	156,800 MHz	156,800 MHz

Table 2.1: Simplex channel

Simplex channels may be used for both ship-to-ship and ship-to-shore communications subject to the restrictions identified by the regulatory body governing channel usage in the area of operation.

Some channels are designated for duplex operation. A duplex channel is a channel on which a radio transmits on one frequency but receives on another frequency. For example, Channel 24 is a duplex channel. When tuned to Channel 24, a vessel's marine VHF radio transmits on a frequency of 157.200 MHz, but it receives on a frequency of 161.800 MHz as indicated in Table 2.2. It

is convenient to think of the receive frequency as being offset or shifted 4.6 MHz above the transmit frequency on any duplex channel.

Channel	Type	Vessel's Transmit Frequency (MHz)	Vessel's Receive Frequency (MHZ)
24	duplex	157,200 MHz	161,800 MHz

Table 2.2: Duplex channel

Duplex channels may only be used for ship-to-shore communications with authorized coast stations whose transmit and receive frequencies will be opposite to those of the vessel. On a duplex channel, an authorized coast station will receive on the vessel's *transmit* frequency, and transmit on the vessel's *receive* frequency. It should be readily apparent that duplex channels cannot be used for ship-to-ship communications.

Why duplex channels? The marine VHF radios *typically* used by recreational boaters are only capable of *semi-duplex* operation. They are able to transmit on one frequency and receive on another, but they are *incapable of doing both at the same time*. When tuned to a duplex channel, the receiver is automatically *disabled* when the microphone's *push-to-talk* (PTT) *button* is depressed to transmit. Consequently, to the recreational boater, it is irrelevant whether operation is on a duplex channel or on a simplex channel. On the other hand, some marine VHF radios intended for commercial use are capable of *full duplex* operation in which the receiver and the transmitter function simultaneously on duplex channels. A radio operating in full duplex mode continues to receive on one frequency while it transmits on another. This means that full duplex operation is just like having a telephone conversation. This is the advantage afforded by duplex channels; however, only stations using marine VHF radios capable of full duplex operation will have this advantage.

A channel containing the letter 'A' as a suffix (sometimes called an *Alpha* channel) is the simplex counterpart of the duplex channel without the 'A' suffix. For example, Channel 22A is the simplex counterpart of duplex Channel 22. As indicated in Table 2.3, duplex Channel

22 and simplex Channel 22A have the same transmit frequency, but Channel 22 has a shifted receive frequency while 22A does not. On any 'A' channel, the radio both transmits and receives on the transmit frequency of the corresponding duplex channel. Simplex 'A' channels are generally only used in Canada and the United States, and their use is normally not recognized or permitted outside of North America.

Some marine VHF radios adhere to this channel numbering convention to display the simplex 'A' channels in the Canada and United States channel groups differently from their duplex counterparts in the International channel group. For example, these radios would display '22' when the International channel group is selected, and they would display '22A' when either the Canada or United States channel group is specified. This is consistent with the manner in which these channels are designated by Industry Canada and the FCC.

Some other marine VHF radios do not incorporate this distinction into the channel display. In this instance, for example, '22' would be displayed in all three channel groups. This can be a source of confusion to a user comparing a list of channels from an official source to those channels displayed on the radio. It is left to the user to realize that, when the Canada or USA channel group is selected on these radios, the displayed Channel 22 is really simplex Channel 22A based on the U/I/C setting (see table 2.3).

Unique to the Canada channel group are four channel numbers followed by the letter 'B' on which marine VHF radios do not have transmit capability. These channels are used by CCG for *continuous marine broadcasts*.

The 'B' channels may not appear programmed as separate channels on some marine VHF radios since it is not really necessary. CCG marine broadcasts on Channels 25B, 28B and 83B may be received on their duplex channel counterparts: 25, 28 and 83, respectively, in the Canada channel group. CCG broadcasts on Channel 21B may be received on WX8 (see below) or on duplex Channel 21 in the International channel group. The user also has the option to receive Channel 83B broadcasts by tuning to WX9.

Also incorporated into marine VHF radios sold in North America is the ability to receive on ten channels normally designated: WX1, WX2,...,WX10. These are the so-called 'weather channels'.

Channels WX1 to WX7, inclusive, are used by Environment Canada's *Weatheradio* service in Canada and by the National Oceanic & Atmospheric Administration's (NOAA) *National Weather Radio* (NWR) service in the United States. Information concerning current local weather conditions, forecasts, and severe weather watches and warnings is broadcast 24 hours a day on these channels. WX8 (VHF Channel 21B) and WX9 (VHF Channel 83B) are used by the CCG for continuous marine broadcasts. On the West Coast, CCG uses WX1, WX2, and WX3 as well as 21B for their Continuous Marine Broadcasts.

Channel	Vessel's Transmit Frequency (MHz)	Vessel's Receive Frequency (MHZ)	Comments
22	151.100 MHz	161,700 MHz	duplex changel shifted receive **frequency**
22A	157.100 MHZ	157.100 MHz	simplex counterpart

Table 2.3: Channel 22A is the simplex counterpart of duplex Channel 22

2.8 Telephone calling

Coast Guard Radio Facilities

The CCG has discontinued telephone patching on the West Coast. They may discontinue this service throughout the country.

Telephone Company Service

To place a call through a Telephone Company Service: (Commercial arrangements must be made in advance, or the company will not provide this service).

(a) Select a designated telephone company channel.
(b) Depress radio transmit switch for three seconds.
(c) Expect to hear a *ringing* tone.
(d) The operator will answer and direct you.

In Canada, some telephone company services, *do not use* 156.8 MHz (VHF) Channel 16 or 2182 kHz (MF).

For access to a vessel by telephone, contact should be made through the Canadian Coast Guard, unless prior scheduling and arrangements have been made.

Neither CCG nor the telephone company will provide this service, unless the station can provide the correct station information such as the vessel's call sign. Charges apply to this service.

2.9 Radio checks

When requesting a *radio check* from Coast Guard Radio, call the station on one of their working frequencies, requesting the check.

Do not call on Channel 16 or 2182 kHz, as Coast Guard Radio will not provide this service.

Radio checks may also be requested from other vessels. Make a normal call to establish contact, and then switch to a working channel.

Signal checks should take the minimum time required.

Example:
> **VICTORIA COAST GUARD RADIO**
> *This is*
> **SEABIRD**
> *Requesting a radio check*
> *Channel 26*
> **OVER**

2.9.1 Readability scale

1 = Bad (unreadable)
2 = Poor (readable now and then)
3 = Fair (readable but with difficulty)
4 = Good (readable)
5 = Excellent (perfectly readable)

Example:
Signal check, Reading You Four, Out. (or Over)

2.10 Control of communications

In all communication situations, *one* of the stations is the *controlling* station. The controlling station decides the procedural matters.

Controlling stations are defined as follows:
In a Distress situation: the vessel in distress, unless control has been assumed by a more capable station.

In non-distress situations, control is assumed by:
(a) Between two ship stations: the station called,
(b) Between ship and shore stations: the shore station,

Note, very often, the shore station is a Coast Guard Station.

2.11 Priorities

The order of priority for radiocommunications is:

(1) *Distress* communications,

(2) *Urgency* communications,

(3) *Safety* communications,

(4) Communications relative to direction-finding bearings,

(5) Communications relative to the navigation, movement and needs of aircraft engaged in search and rescue operations,

(6) Messages containing exclusively meteorological (weather) observations destined to an official meteorological office,

(7) Communications related to the application of the United Nations Charter,

(8) Service messages relative to the working of the radiocommunications service or to messages that have been previously transmitted,

(9) All other communications.

Figure 2.5: Canadian Coast Guard vessels

Maritime Radio Course
Student's Notes

module 1

Section 3

3.0 Distress communication

Distress communication should be conducted in accordance with the procedures outlined below. These procedures shall not prevent a *vessel in distress* from making use of any means at its disposal to attract attention, make known its position and obtain assistance.

3.1 Priority

The Distress call shall have absolute priority over all other transmissions. All stations which hear it shall *immediately* cease any transmission capable of interfering with Distress traffic and shall continue to listen on the frequency used for the Distress call.

3.2 Frequencies to be used

A Distress call and message from a ship should be first transmitted on the Distress, Safety and Calling frequency of 2182 kHz (MF), or VHF Channel 16.

Coast Guard Radio Stations do not monitor G.R.S. (General Radio Service commonly called Citizen's Band) Channel 9.

3.3 Distress signal

In Marine radio communications, the Distress signal consists of the word *Mayday*. The Distress signal *indicates* that the station sending the signal or a person on board is:

(a) Threatened by *grave and imminent danger* and requires immediate assistance, or
(b) Aware that a ship, aircraft or other vehicle is threatened by *grave and imminent danger* and requires immediate assistance.

3.4 Distress call

The Distress call and message shall only be sent on the authority of the person in command of the station.

The Distress call should comprise:

(a) The alarm signal (if the vessel is fitted with this equipment),
(b) The distress signal *Mayday* spoken three times,
(c) The words *This is*,
(d) The name of the vessel in Distress spoken three times. (There may be more than one vessel with the same name; be sure to include a specific form of identification—eg., licence or registration number).

The International Radiotelephone Alarm signal consists of a continuous transmission of two audio tones that produces a *warbling* sound for a period of at least thirty seconds, but not exceeding one minute. The purpose of this signal is to alert stations guarding 2182 kHz (MF) or VHF Channel 16, that a Distress call and message is to follow. Coast Guard Radio Stations use this signal on 2182 kHz (MF) and VHF Channel 16 prior to issuing a *Mayday Relay*.

The Distress call shall not be addressed to a particular station and acknowledgement of receipt shall not be given *before* the Distress message is sent.

3.5 Distress message

The Distress call shall be followed as soon as possible by the *Distress message. (The Distress call and Distress message will normally be sent together in a single transmission.)*

The Distress message shall be comprised of:

(a) The Distress signal *Mayday,*
(b) The name of the vessel in distress (once),
(c) Particulars of its *position* (as accurately as possible),
(d) *Nature* of the distress and kind of assistance required, (what has happened),
(e) A description of the vessel in distress,
(f) The *number of persons* on board and *injuries,* (if applicable),

(g) Any other information which might facilitate rescue, ("preparing to abandon ship with lifejackets"),

(h) The *name* of the vessel,

(i) The word *over.*

3.5.1 Example of a Distress call and message from a ship

MAYDAY MAYDAY MAYDAY
This is
SEADOG SEADOG SEADOG

MAYDAY SEADOG
Position two miles south of Merry Island
Have struck a log and taking on water
Engine seized
Two seven foot Bayliner, white with orange stripe
Three people on board, one injured
Preparing to abandon ship with lifejackets
no dinghy,
SEADOG
OVER

3.5.2 Repetition of a Distress message

The Distress message shall be repeated at intervals by the vessel in distress until an answer is received or until it is no longer feasible to continue. The intervals between repetitions of the Distress message shall be sufficiently long to allow time for stations which have received the message to reply.

When a vessel in distress receives no answer to its Distress call, sent on the distress frequencies 2182 kHz (MF) or VHF Channel 16, the Distress call and message should be repeated on any other available frequency on which attention might be attracted (i.e. ship-to-ship or ship-to-shore).

3.6 Action by other ships

3.6.1 Acknowledgement of receipt of a Distress message

Vessels which receive a Distress message from a vessel in their vicinity and are *able to render assistance* should defer acknowledgement for a short interval so

that a Coast Guard Radio Station may acknowledge receipt of the Distress message first, interference free.

The Coast Guard Radio Station operator, upon acknowledging receipt of a Distress message, may take one or more of the following actions, depending on the situation:

(a) Confirm information such as the distressed vessel's position, description, seaworthiness, number of persons on board, etc.,

(b) Contact the Rescue Co-ordination Centre (RCC) with details of the *incident*. (At the time of writing, RCC staff decide which available Search and Rescue facilities will be dispatched during an incident),

(c) *Patch* RCC staff into Coast Guard Radio Station facilities to allow direct communications between rcc and the vessel in distress,

(d) Transmit a *Mayday Relay* or a Marine Information Bulletin requesting other vessels in the area to "assist the vessel in distress and advise".

Vessels receiving a Distress message that *has been acknowledged* by a Coast Guard Radio Station and are able to render assistance almost immediately should proceed towards the distress vessel's location while monitoring the distress channel. Once the Coast Guard Radio Station has requested assistance from other vessels, a call to the CG Radio Station stating your speed and estimated time of arrival to the vessel in distress may be made. Care should be taken to ensure interference is not caused to traffic between the distress vessel and the CG Radio Station, or rescue vessel(s) closer to it.

Figure 3.1: CCG Hovercraft

On the other hand, vessels which receive a Distress message that *has not been acknowledged,* after a short interval by a Coast Guard Radio Station or other ship, and are able to render assistance, shall acknowledge the Distress message in the following form:

(a) The Distress signal *Mayday* (once),
(b) The name of the vessel in Distress (three times),
(c) The words *This is,*
(d) The name of the *vessel acknowledging receipt* (three times),
(e) The words *Received Mayday,*
(f) Any information that might be pertinent to the vessel in distress, (speed and estimated time of arrival (ETA) to the distress vessel's location),
(g) The word *over* (the vessel in distress may wish to exchange further traffic with the station acknowledging the distress message).

Example of acknowledgement of receipt of a Distress message by ship (other than Coast Guard Radio)

(the vessel Moonbeamer is able to render assistance)

MAYDAY
SEADOG SEADOG SEADOG
This is
MOONBEAMER MOONBEAMER MOONBEAMER
RECEIVED MAYDAY
I am located approximately one mile south and proceeding to your location to render assistance eta approximately one zero minutes
MOONBEAMER
OVER

3.6.2 Relay of a Distress message

Vessels which receive a Distress message and *are not in a position to render assistance quickly,* i.e. more than twenty minutes away should note all the pertinent details such as: distressed vessel's name, location, nature of distress, description of vessel, number of people on board, etc., in a *Radio Log* while listening for an acknowledgement. This action will reduce or eliminate the possibility of transmitting inaccurate information concerning the distressed vessel should there be a requirement to *relay* the distress message.

Figure 3.2: Response by ship station able to render assistance

If no acknowledgement of receipt is made by a CG Radio Station, or other ship station closer to the Distress location, after a short interval of time, the Distress message should be acknowledged as set out in Section 3.6.1. This is to assure the vessel in distress that the Distress message has been received by another station. The vessel in distress should then be told that the message will be relayed.

A Distress message repeated by a vessel other than the vessel in distress shall transmit a signal comprised of:

(a) The signal *Mayday Relay* spoken three times,
(b) The words *This is,*
(c) The name of the vessel *relaying* the message (three times),
(d) The distress signal *Mayday* (once),
(e) The name of the vessel in distress (once),
(f) The particulars of the message, such as the Distress vessel's location, nature of Distress, description, number of persons on board, etc.

Any Station in the maritime mobile service that has heard a Distress message that has not been *acknowledged* after a short interval of time *must* acknowledge and render assistance or acknowledge and relay the message. In some cases, the vessel relaying the Distress message may turn out to be the closest vessel to the Distress location, and be requested to act as a rescue vessel.

Example of a Relay by another ship

Prosperous is unable to render assistance, but can relay message

MAYDAY
DOLPHIN DOLPHIN DOLPHIN
This is
PROSPEROUS PROSPEROUS
PROSPEROUS

RECEIVED MAYDAY
*Unable to assist, **STANDBY**, will relay for you*
MAYDAY RELAY MAYDAY RELAY
MAYDAY RELAY

This is
PROSPEROUS PROSPEROUS
PROSPEROUS

MAYDAY DOLPHIN
Is located at the Northwest end of Gambier Island
Has struck a deadhead and taking on water
She is a two two foot Fibreform, white hull with blue cabin
Four people on board, no injuries
They are preparing to abandon ship with lifejackets, no dinghy
PROSPEROUS
OVER

The importance of recording the details of a Distress message in a Radio Log is especially apparent during a *Mayday Relay*.

3.6.3 Further action

Vessel(s) that has (have) acknowledged receipt of a Distress message, or relayed a Distress message, shall take the following additional action if applicable.

(a) Contact the nearest Coast Guard Radio Station if this station is not aware of the distress situation.
(b) Forward information to Search and Rescue.
(c) Cease all transmissions which may interfere with traffic between Search and Rescue stations and the vessel in distress.

3.7 Distress traffic

Distress traffic consists of all transmissions relative to the immediate assistance required by the ship in distress. Essentially, all transmissions made after the initial distress call may be considered as **Distress traffic.** In distress traffic, the distress signal *Mayday*, spoken once, shall precede **all** transmissions. This procedure is intended to alert stations not aware of the initial distress call and now monitoring the distress channel—that traffic heard relates to a distress situation.

Any station in the maritime mobile service which has knowledge of distress traffic, and cannot itself assist the station in distress, shall nevertheless follow such traffic until it is evident that assistance is being provided. Until a message is received indicating that normal working may be resumed (cancellation of Distress), all stations which are aware of the Distress traffic, and which are not taking part in it, are forbidden to transmit on the frequencies on which the Distress traffic is taking place.

3.7.1 Control of Distress traffic

Initially, of course, the control of Distress traffic is the responsibility of the vessel in distress, or of the station which sent the *Distress message* (i.e. a relaying station). However, these stations may delegate the control of Distress traffic to another station, such as a Coast Guard station. **During most incidents,** a Coast Guard stations will, if radio communications are satisfactory, assume control of the distress traffic.

3.8 Imposition of silence

The station in distress, or any station in the immediate vicinity may impose silence on a particular station or stations in the area if interference is being caused to distress traffic.

The station in distress shall use the expression "*Seelonce Mayday*", while other stations use "*Seelonce Distress*".

3.8.1 Example of a specific station by the vessel in distress

Seadog is the vessel in distress. Sunflight is causing interference to distress traffic

MAYDAY
SUNFLIGHT SUNFLIGHT SUNFLIGHT
This is
SEADOG SEADOG SEADOG

SEELONCE MAYDAY
Distress traffic in progress
STOP TRANSMITTING
OUT

3.8.2 Example of "All Stations" by vessel other than vessel in distress

Stations other than the vessel in distress shall impose silence during a Distress situation, using the expression *Seelonce Distress.*

MAYDAY
ALL STATIONS ALL STATIONS
ALL STATIONS
This is
MOONBEAMER MOONBEAMER
MOONBEAMER

SEELONCE DISTRESS
OUT

3.8.3 Example of "All Stations" by a Coast Guard Radio Station that is the controlling station

MAYDAY
ALL STATIONS ALL STATIONS
ALL STATIONS
This is
VANCOUVER COAST GUARD RADIO
VANCOUVER COAST GUARD RADIO
VANCOUVER COAST GUARD RADIO
SEELONCE DISTRESS
Cease Transmitting
VANCOUVER COAST GUARD RADIO
OUT

Should radio silence be imposed during a distress situation, **all transmissions shall cease immediately**, except from those stations involved in distress traffic.

3.9 Cancellation of distress

When a vessel is no longer in distress, or when it is no longer necessary to observe radio silence (i.e. rescue operation has concluded)—the vessel that was in distress, the rescue vessel, or the station that controlled distress traffic, shall transmit a message addressed to *All Stations,* on the distress frequency(ies) advising that the distress traffic has ended.

The proper procedure for cancelling a distress message is:

(a) The distress signal *Mayday* (once),
(b) The words *"All Stations"* (three times),
(c) The words *"This is,"*
(d) The name of the station transmitting the message (three times),
(e) The filing time of the message,
(f) The name of the vessel in distress (once),
(g) The words *"Seelonce Feenee,"*
(h) A short, plain language description of why the distress situation is being cancelled,
(i) The name of the station cancelling the distress,
(j) The word *out*.

The procedure outlined above is mainly for the benefit of other stations for the resumption of regular service on the distress frequencies. To **ensure** that Search and Rescue stations are advised that a station is no longer in distress, a normal call to the nearest Coast Guard Radio Station, detailing the reasons for cancelling the distress call **must** be made.

3.9.1 Example of cancellation of distress (by rescue vessel)

MAYDAY
ALL STATIONS ALL STATIONS
ALL STATIONS
This is
MOONBEAMER MOONBEAMER
MOONBEAMER
One eight three zero Pacific Standard

SEADOG
SEELONCE FEENEE

All three persons safe on board this vessel. Seadog has sunk. We are transporting crew to Sechelt.

MOONBEAMER
OUT

Maritime Radio Course
Student's Notes

Section 4

4.0 Urgency communications

4.1 Priority

The Urgency signal has priority over all other communications, except Distress. Stations which hear the Urgency signal shall continue to listen for *at least three minutes* on the frequency on which the signal is heard. If no Urgency message has been heard, the stations may resume normal service. All stations which hear the Urgency signal must take care *not* to interfere with the Urgency message which follows it.

Provided that the Urgency message is not addressed to *All Stations,* stations that wish to communicate on frequencies other than those used for the transmission of the Urgency message may continue normal work without interruption.

4.2 Frequencies to be used

The Urgency signal and message following it shall be sent on the Distress, Safety and Calling frequencies of 2182 kHz (MF) and/or 156.8 MHz (VHF) Channel 16.

4.3 Urgency signal

The Urgency signal is *Pan Pan* spoken three times. It is sent before the call.

The Urgency signal indicates that the station calling has a very urgent message to transmit concerning the **safety of a ship, aircraft or other vehicle or the safety of a person.**

When used by a ship station, the message preceded by the Urgency signal may be addressed to *All Stations* or to a specific station, and shall be used only on the authority of the person in command.

4.4 Urgency message

The *Urgency* signal shall be followed by a message giving further information of the incident which necessitated the use of the signal. The message shall be in plain language.

4.4.1 Examples of Urgency calls and messages

To All Stations:
> **PAN PAN PAN PAN PAN PAN**
> **ALL STATIONS ALL STATIONS**
> **ALL STATIONS**
> *This is*
> **WILLOW WILLOW WILLOW**
>
> *Located two miles due west of Sea Island*
> *Have damaged rudder, unable to steer*
> *Not taking on water*
> *Am in no immediate danger*
> *Request tow to nearest Marina*
> **WILLOW**
> **OVER**

To a specific station:
> **PAN PAN PAN PAN PAN PAN**
> **HALIFAX COAST GUARD RADIO HALIFAX**
> **COAST GUARD RADIO**
> **HALIFAX COAST GUARD RADIO**
> *This is*
> **NORTH WIND NORTH WIND NORTH WIND**
>
> *Position one zero miles south of Halifax*
> *Have injured crew member requiring medical attention*
> *Engine stalled, unable to restart*
> *Request helicopter air lift*
> **NORTH WIND**
> **OVER**

4.4.2 Receipt of an Urgency Message.

Upon receiving an Urgency message, your response would be similar to that for a Distress call. First, give the Coast Guard a chance to reply. If they do not reply, you should do so.

Example of acknowledgement of receipt of an Urgency message by ship (other than Coast Guard Radio)

The vessel Moonbeamer is replying.

> **Pan Pan**
> **SEADOG SEADOG SEADOG**
> *This is*
> **MOONBEAMER MOONBEAMER**
> **MOONBEAMER**
> **RECEIVED** message
> I am located approximately one mile south and proceeding to your location to render assistance
> ETA approximately one zero minutes
> **MOONBEAMER**
> **OVER**

4.5 Cancellation of urgency

When the Urgency signal has been sent before transmitting a message addressed to *All Stations* which calls for action by stations receiving the message, the station responsible for its transmission shall cancel it as soon as it knows that action is no longer necessary.

The cancellation shall be addressed to *All Stations*.

> **PAN PAN**
> **ALL STATIONS ALL STATIONS**
> **ALL STATIONS**
> *This is*
> **WILLOW WILLOW WILLOW**
> *Under tow to Marina*
> **URGENCY ENDED**
> **WILLOW**
> **OUT**

A normal call to the nearest Coast Guard Radio Station, advising them that you are no longer in an urgent situation, **must** be made.

1

Maritime Radio Course
Student's Notes

Section 5

5.0 Safety communications

5.1 Priority

The *Safety* signal has priority over all other communications, except Distress and Urgency.

All stations hearing the Safety signal shall shift to the working frequency indicated in the call, and listen until they are satisfied that the message is of no concern to them.

All stations that hear the Safety signal must take care *not* to interfere with the message which follows it. No transmission shall be made that may interfere with these stations.

5.2 Safety signal

In marine radio, the Safety signal is the word *Sécurité* spoken three times. It is sent before the call. The safety signal indicates that the station calling is about to transmit a message containing an important navigational or meteorological warning.

5.3 Procedures

The Safety signal and call shall be sent on the international distress frequencies of 2182 kHz (MF) and/or VHF Channel 16. The *Safety* message which follows the call should be sent on a suitable working frequency. An announcement to this effect shall be made at the end of the call.

In the Maritime Mobile Service, safety calls and messages shall generally be addressed to *All Stations*. In some cases, however, they may be addressed to a particular station (i.e. Coast Guard Radio Station). When a safety call is addressed to a CG Radio Station, the message should follow on a Coast Guard working frequency.

Safety signals and calls may be transmitted at any time on VHF Channel 16. For vessels fitted with 2182 kHz (MF), the safety signal and call should be transmitted at the end of the first available silence period, and the message transmitted immediately after the silence period, on a suitable working frequency.

Meteorological and navigational warning messages which contain information about *imminent danger to marine navigation* **must** be transmitted without delay and repeated as indicated above, at the end of the first silence period which follows:

(a) On VHF, a suitable working frequency is Channel 06 as it is designated *Intership*. Most vessels equipped with VHF are fitted with Channel 06.

(b) On MF, a suitable working frequency can be either 2638 kHz or 2738 kHz as these frequencies are designated *Intership* for all types of vessels (towing, fishing and pleasure craft).

5.4 Example of a Safety call

The Safety call shall be sent only on the authority of the person in command of the station. The Safety call is made on Channel 16.

> **SÉCURITÉ SÉCURITÉ SÉCURITÉ**
> **ALL STATIONS ALL STATIONS**
> **ALL STATIONS**
> *This is*
> **GLENAYRE GLENAYRE GLENAYRE**
>
> *Safety message concerning Cabot Head area to follow Channel 06*
> **GLENAYRE**
> **OUT**

All stations hearing the above Safety call would then switch to Channel 06 where the following call will be made.

SÉCURITÉ SÉCURITÉ SÉCURITÉ
ALL STATIONS ALL STATIONS
ALL STATIONS

This is
GLENAYRE GLENAYRE GLENAYRE

Oil barge broken loose and adrift five miles due east
Cabot Head Light
Menace to navigation
GLENAYRE
OUT

The above example is applicable for vessels fitted with VHF radio equipment.

Maritime
Radio Course
Student's Notes

Section 6

module 1

6.0 Distress simulations

6.1 Involvement with Canadian Coast Guard Radio Stations

The student should be aware that the majority of Distress situations are answered immediately by a Coast Guard Radio Station.

The following examples will illustrate how Coast Guard Radio Stations respond, and the actions taken in Distress traffic by the other vessels involved.

In these situations, Coast Guard Radio will *always* become the *controlling* station.

Scenario
The vessel *Morning Star* has struck a reef at the southwest side of Bowen Island. It is taking on water and sinking. Three people are on board. Vessel is a 26-foot Bayliner, white with brown trim. The vessel has no dinghy, although it carries personal flotation devices for all persons on board.

6.2 Distress call and message

MAYDAY MAYDAY MAYDAY
This is
MORNING STAR MORNING STAR MORNING STAR

MAYDAY
MORNING STAR
Position southwest of Bowen Island.
Have struck a reef, taking on water, sinking.
Vessel is a two six foot Bayliner, white with brown trim.
Three persons on board. Preparing to abandon ship.
No dinghy; persons aboard are wearing lifejackets.
MORNING STAR
OVER

6.2.1 Acknowledgement of Mayday by Canadian Coast Guard radio

MAYDAY
MORNING STAR MORNING STAR MORNING STAR
This is
VANCOUVER COAST GUARD RADIO
VANCOUVER COAST GUARD RADIO
VANCOUVER COAST GUARD RADIO

RECEIVED MAYDAY
(Example reply message)
Will attempt to locate a nearby vessel to assist you.
Standby
OVER

6.2.2 Distress relay

MAYDAY RELAY MAYDAY RELAY MAYDAY RELAY
This is
VANCOUVER COAST GUARD RADIO
VANCOUVER COAST GUARD RADIO
VANCOUVER COAST GUARD RADIO

MAYDAY
MORNING STAR
has struck a reef on the southwest side of Bowen Island, is taking on water and is sinking.
The **MORNING STAR** *is a two six foot Bayliner, white with brown trim, three persons on board, preparing to abandon ship. Vessel has no dinghy, but persons are wearing lifejackets. Any vessels in the area respond,*
giving position and estimated time of arrival.
VANCOUVER COAST GUARD RADIO
OVER

The vessel *Seafoam* is just leaving Plumpers Cove and is approximately 20 minutes from the *Morning Star*'s position and is able to assist. *Seafoam* responds to Coast Guard Radio.

6.2.3 Acknowledgement/assist by other station

MAYDAY
VANCOUVER COAST GUARD RADIO
VANCOUVER COAST GUARD RADIO
VANCOUVER COAST GUARD RADIO
This is
SEAFOAM SEAFOAM SEAFOAM
RECEIVED MAYDAY
Position **PLUMPERS COVE, ETA**
(Estimated Time of Arrival) to **MORNING STAR**
two zero minutes or position
PLUMPERS COVE, proceeding to **MORNING**
STAR
ETA *two zero minutes*
SEAFOAM
OVER

6.2.4 Distress traffic

MAYDAY
SEAFOAM
This is
VANCOUVER COAST GUARD RADIO
Roger, understand you are at Plumpers Cove,
proceeding to **MORNING STAR,**
ETA *two zero minutes.*
Advise this station when you are on scene.
OVER

MAYDAY
VANCOUVER COAST GUARD RADIO
This is
SEAFOAM
WILCO
OUT

During the lull in Distress communications, a number of vessels break *radio silence* by calling other vessels.

6.2.5 Impose silence by controlling station

MAYDAY
ALL STATIONS ALL STATIONS
ALL STATIONS
This is
VANCOUVER COAST GUARD RADIO
VANCOUVER COAST GUARD RADIO
VANCOUVER COAST GUARD RADIO
SEELONCE DISTRESS. *Distress traffic is in progress, stop transmitting.*
VANCOUVER COAST GUARD RADIO
OUT

6.2.6 Impose silence by vessel other than vessel in distress

The vessel *Misty* continues to call on the Distress channel. *Seafoam* imposes *radio silence* on *Misty*.

MAYDAY
MISTY MISTY MISTY
This is
SEAFOAM SEAFOAM SEAFOAM
SEELONCE DISTRESS. *Distress traffic is in progress, stop transmitting.*
SEAFOAM
OUT

6.2.7 Distress traffic on scene

The vessel *Seafoam* arrives on scene at *Morning Star*. The vessel has sunk. *Seafoam* recovers all three persons; there are no injuries. The *Seafoam* is proceeding to Fisherman's Cove.

MAYDAY
VANCOUVER COAST GUARD RADIO
VANCOUVER COAST GUARD RADIO
VANCOUVER COAST GUARD RADIO
This is
SEAFOAM SEAFOAM SEAFOAM
On scene, I have recovered all three persons from **MORNING STAR.** *There are no injuries.*
Vessel Morning Star has sunk.
Transporting the three persons to Fisherman's Cove.

SEAFOAM
OVER

MAYDAY
SEAFOAM
This is
VANCOUVER COAST GUARD RADIO
ROGER, *understand you have recovered all three persons*
from **MORNING STAR,** *no injuries.*
Vessel has sunk. Understand proceeding to
Fisherman's Cove, report your arrival.
OVER

MAYDAY
VANCOUVER COAST GUARD RADIO
This is
SEAFOAM
ROGER. *That is correct*
OUT

Distress traffic and the Distress incident are now concluded. The controlling station will now *cancel* the Distress, indicating normal working may resume on the Distress and Calling channel.

6.2.8 Cancellation of distress by controlling station

MAYDAY
ALL STATIONS ALL STATIONS
ALL STATIONS
This is
VANCOUVER COAST GUARD RADIO
VANCOUVER COAST GUARD RADIO
VANCOUVER COAST GUARD RADIO
Time 161200P
SEELONCE FEENEE
All three persons recovered. The vessel
MORNING STAR *has sunk.*
VANCOUVER COAST GUARD RADIO
OUT

6.3 Homework study

6.3.1 Distress call and message from a ship

The following examples of calls are to be used for homework study.

MAYDAY MAYDAY MAYDAY
This is
SEADOG SEADOG SEADOG
MAYDAY SEADOG
Position, two miles south of Merry Island
Have struck a log and taking on water
Engine seized
Two seven foot Bayliner, white with orange stripe
Three people on board, one injured
Preparing to abandon ship with lifejackets, no dinghy.
SEADOG
OVER

6.3.2 Acknowledgement by another ship

No acknowledgements from a Coast Guard Radio Station or other ships have been made after a short interval of time; *Moonbeamer* is able to render assistance.

MAYDAY
SEADOG SEADOG SEADOG
This is
MOONBEAMER MOONBEAMER
MOONBEAMER
RECEIVED MAYDAY
I am located approximately one mile south and proceeding to your location to render assistance
ETA approximately one zero minutes
MOONBEAMER
OVER

6.3.3 Distress traffic

The rescue vessel *Moonbeamer* is proceeding towards the Distress vessel *Seadog*.

> **MAYDAY**
> **SEADOG**
> *This is*
> **MOONBEAMER**
> *I am approximately one quarter mile from your location.*
> *Confirm your vessel colours as white with orange stripe.*
> **OVER**

The Distress vessel *Seadog* responds to rescue vessel *Moonbeamer*.

> **MAYDAY**
> **MOONBEAMER**
> *This is*
> **SEADOG**
> **ROGER,** *That is correct.*
> **OUT**

6.3.4 Imposition of silence

On a Specific Station by the Vessel in Distress

The vessel *Sunflight*, no call sign stated, is causing interference to Distress traffic.

> **MAYDAY**
> **SUNFLIGHT SUNFLIGHT SUNFLIGHT**
> *This is*
> **SEADOG SEADOG SEADOG**
> **SEELONCE MAYDAY**
> **OUT**

On "All Stations" by Vessel Other Than the Vessel in Distress

> **MAYDAY**
> **ALL STATIONS ALL STATIONS**
> **ALL STATIONS**

> *This is*
> **MOONBEAMER MOONBEAMER**
> **MOONBEAMER**
> **SEELONCE DISTRESS**
> **OUT**

On "All Stations" by a Coast Guard Radio Station

> **MAYDAY**
> **ALL STATIONS ALL STATIONS**
> **ALL STATIONS**
> *This is*
> **VANCOUVER COAST GUARD RADIO**
> **VANCOUVER COAST GUARD RADIO**
> **VANCOUVER COAST GUARD RADIO**
> **SEELONCE DISTRESS**
> *Stop Transmitting*
> **VANCOUVER COAST GUARD RADIO**
> **OUT**

6.3.5 Cancellation of distress

By Rescue Vessel

> **MAYDAY**
> **ALL STATIONS ALL STATIONS**
> **ALL STATIONS**
> *This is*
> **MOONBEAMER MOONBEAMER**
> **MOONBEAMER**
> *One eight three zero Pacific Standard Time*
> **SEADOG**
> **SEELONCE FEENEE**
> *All three persons safe on board this vessel.*
> SEADOG has sunk.
> *We are transporting the crew to Sechelt.*
> **MOONBEAMER**
> **OUT**

By Coast Guard Radio Station

> **MAYDAY**
> **ALL STATIONS ALL STATIONS**
> **ALL STATIONS**

This is
VANCOUVER COAST GUARD RADIO
VANCOUVER COAST GUARD RADIO
VANCOUVER COAST GUARD RADIO
One eight four five Pacific Standard Time
SEADOG
SEELONCE FEENEE
Resume Normal Transmission
VANCOUVER COAST GUARD RADIO
OUT

6.3.6 Distress call and message

MAYDAY MAYDAY MAYDAY
This is
DOLPHIN DOLPHIN DOLPHIN
MAYDAY DOLPHIN
Position Northwest end Gambier Island
Have struck a deadhead, taking on water
Two two foot Fibreform, white hull with blue cabin
Four people on board, no injuries
Preparing to abandon ship with lifejackets, no dinghy.
DOLPHIN
OVER

No acknowledgement from a Coast Guard Radio Station or other ships has been made after a short interval of time.

6.3.7 Relay by another vessel

The vessel Prosperous is unable to render assistance but can relay the Distress message.

MAYDAY
DOLPHIN DOLPHIN DOLPHIN
This is
PROSPEROUS PROSPEROUS PROSPEROUS
RECEIVED MAYDAY
Unable to assist, **STANDBY**, *will relay for you*
MAYDAY RELAY MAYDAY RELAY
MAYDAY RELAY
This is
PROSPEROUS PROSPEROUS PROSPEROUS
MAYDAY DOLPHIN
Is located at the Northwest end of Gambier Island
Has struck a deadhead and is taking on water
She is a two two foot Fibreform, white hull with blue cabin
Four people on board; no injuries. They are preparing to abandon ship with lifejackets; no dinghy.
PROSPEROUS

OVER

The importance of recording the details of a Distress message in a *Radio Log* is especially apparent during a *Mayday Relay*.

1

Maritime
Radio Course
Student's Notes

Section 7

7.0 Additional information

7.1 Alarm signals

Radio operators in the Maritime Mobile Service should be aware of the specialized equipment that may be used in distress situations to help facilitate rescue.

Some of the more common emergency equipment is listed below.

7.1.1 Radiotelephone alarm

The international radiotelephone alarm signal consists of a repetitive transmission of two audio tones that produce a *warbling* sound. This lasts for a period of at least thirty seconds, but does not exceed one minute.

The purpose of this signal is to alert stations that a distress call is to follow. This alarm signal is to precede a distress signal, call and message, or a Mayday Relay from a Coast Guard Radio Station.

VHF radio equipment on pleasure craft is generally *not fitted* with a radiotelephone alarm signal-generating device, but equipment used by commmerical vessels and the Coast Guard is so equipped.

7.1.2 Navigational warning signal

The navigational warning signal is transmitted from a Coast Station for a period of fifteen seconds *before* vital navigational warnings on the medium frequency of 2182 kHz.

The navigational warning signal consists of an interrupted tone frequency of 2.2 kHz. The duration of each tone and interruption is 250 milliseconds (a quarter of a second). The purpose of this signal is to attract the attention of the operator that a message concerning a navigational warning is to follow. Navigational warnings can be issued for *weather, storm, hurricane, safety notices,* etc.

7.1.3 Emergency Position Indicating Radio Beacon (EPIRB)

Marine EPIRBs are designed to be carried aboard ships and survival craft and are intended to be used in *emergency* situations. EPIRB's are to help determination of the position of survivors in Search and Rescue operations. When an EPIRB is activated, either automatically or manually, it transmits a *distinct* Distress signal in the very high frequency band (VHF) to alert Coast Guard and Search and Rescue (SAR) authorities that a *marine distress incident* has occurred. It also enables sar authorities, ships and aircraft to locate the position of the unit emitting the Distress signal.

There are various types of EPIRBs. Some are capable of floating free of a sinking ship and are activated automatically. Others are manually activated and deployed, or else attached to personnel, or the survival craft. All new units are equipped with a strobe light.

The Distress signal is transmitted on 406.025 MHz to SAR authorities through satellite systems. Older EPIRBs used the aircraft emergency frequency of 121.5 but satellites no longer receive that frequency so those EPIRBs are no longer useable. Some EPIRBs do put out a weak homing signal on 121.5 but the important signal that satellites look for is referred to as 406 MHz. The 121.5 homing signal may be used by Search and Rescue vessels and aircraft.

The EPIRB signal consists of two audio tones alternating to give a warbling effect.

EPIRB's may or may not incorporate a GPS. It is strongly recommended that your unit have an integrated GPS as these units will ensure a much quicker search and rescue response.

7.1.4 Emergency Position Indicating Buoy (EPIB)

Buoys that must be carried by towing vessels (tugs) of more than 5 gross tons (with some exceptions) are known as EPIBs. The EPIB is radar reflective, painted fluorescent orange and marked in black letters with the *name of the vessel* and the following:

Do Not Remove Buoy
Sunken Ship
Report Position to Coast Guard.
This device is attached to the vessel with an anchor line of not less than 914 metres in length, and the buoy is equipped with a *flashing amber light* that comes into operation when the buoy is afloat.

7.2 General electronic information

7.2.1 Lead acid storage batteries

Power for electronic equipment on small vessels is almost universally supplied by lead acid storage batteries. These are used because they may be recharged and serve as a reservoir of power. Some batteries are of 'sealed' construction.

Some have a 'gel' instead of liquid acid. They are spill proof and are usually installed in vessels that are likely to tip during use, e.g., PWCs, hydroplanes, etc.

Maintenance

To insure maximum service from a battery, it is necessary to maintain it as follows:

NOTE, on sealed batteries, it may be difficult or impossible to check the electrolyte level or to add fluid. Gel batteries do not need to have the level checked.

(a) The battery must be stored in a cool, dry, well-ventilated area especially constructed for this purpose.

(b) The terminals of the battery must be kept clean and the connections secure. A thin application of petroleum jelly to the terminals will eliminate corrosion.

(c) The electrolyte (battery fluid) must be maintained at the appropriate level. This level will keep the plates (visible through the opening) covered to a depth of approximately one cm. Only distilled water may be used to 'top up' the level. *Never add acid to a battery 'top up'!*

(d) The charge stored in the battery must be kept near its upper limit. This can be checked by a hydrometer to obtain a reading of the charge by indicating the specific gravity of the electrolyte. This may not be possible with a sealed battery and hydrometers do not work with Gel batteries. The charge may also be checked by means of a voltmeter specifically designed for testing batteries.

(e) If the battery is to be stored or left unused for an extended period of time, it should periodically be checked and maintained in a fully charged state.

(f) Batteries should not be charged at a rate greater than 20% of the ampere hour capacity of the battery, and it should have a charger that will taper off as full charge is reached. Constant trickle charging and rapid charging can be harmful to a battery. Connect the charger to the battery terminals before connecting to 110V power supply.

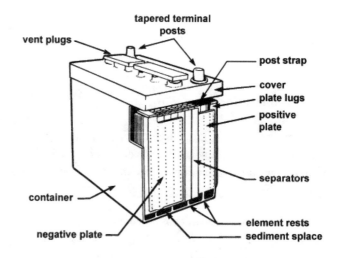

Figure 7.1: Marine battery

Caution

Hazards pertaining to the use and maintenance of batteries require the following precautions:

(a) The battery must be securely restrained to prevent movement.
(b) The battery must be protected from falling objects.
(c) Ventilation of the battery compartment will ensure that there will be no accumulation of the explosive gases associated with charging.
(d) Smoking must not be permitted in the vicinity of the battery, particularly during the charging process.
(e) Care must be taken while checking the electrolyte level as it is an extremely corrosive fluid which can cause severe burns to the body or damage to clothing and other objects.

7.2.2 Wiring

Of equal importance to the operation of the electronic equipment on board any vessel is the distribution of the power. This is achieved with the use of *wiring*.

A 50 ohm impedance coax cable is required for VHF antenna installations. The most commonly used are RG-8X or RG-58AU. RG-8X is preferable.

Maintenance
Among the numerous tasks required to keep the wiring in good condition are the following:

(a) The wiring must be secure and protected from chafing.
(b) Connections must be kept clean and tight.
(c) Connections intended to be disconnected as a normal procedure are particularly vulnerable to damage and, for this reason, must receive frequent attention.

Coupling Ring   Adapter   Adapter Washer   Plug Sub-assembly

1. Cut the end of the coax cable off square.

2. Carefully remove 1-1/16 (2.7 cm) of the vinyl jacket from the end of the cable with a sharp knife, not a razor blade. Do not nick the braid.

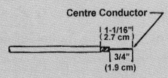

Centre Conductor

1-1/16" (2.7 cm)

3/4" (1.9 cm)

3. Remove 3/4 in (1.9 cm) of both the braid and centre conductor insulation from the end of the cable. Do not nick centre conductor.

4. Slide the coupling ring and then the adapter onto the coax, well up out of your way.

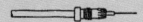

5. Position the adapter flush with the end of the coax.

6. Fold the braid back over the adapter, and press it down over the body of the adapter.

Adapter washer

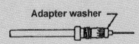

7. Slip the adapter washer over the centre conductor and its insulation so the washer butts against the braid.

8. Screw the plug sub-assembly fully on the adapter (you may need to use pliers).

Contact Pin

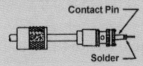

Solder

9. Using a low heat soldering iron (40 watt), put a drop of solder in the end of the contact pin. Use enough to fill the tip of the contact pin.

10. Clip the excess centre conductor wire off with a pair of wire cutters.

11. Screw the coupling ring onto the plug sub-assembly until it spins freely.

Figure 7.2: Assembling PL-259 connector on coax

(d) Use *soldered* or properly *crimped* connections.

(e) Fuses which fail in service should be replaced only with those of equal value. Failed fuses may be an indication of a serious fault; and use of an oversize replacement could cause further damage. Repetitive *blowing* of a fuse certainly indicates a serious problem.

(f) Maintenance of the radio antenna should include adjustment to a vertical position, if required, and periodic checking of the cable and its connections.

7.3 Alternative radio services

The Maritime Radio Course covers the requirements of operating in the Marine Band Radio Service. There are other services which may be of interest to pleasure boaters.

7.3.1 General Radio Service (GRS)

This is commonly known by its American designation, *Citizen's Band (CB)*.

GRS provides a low-cost communication link with a minimum of operational red tape. It is very good for the use of groups of vessels travelling together, or for direct communication between a vessel and an associated land station, such as home or office.

Students should be aware of the following drawbacks:

(a) Power, and hence effective distance, is very limited.

(b) No telephone service is possible.

(c) Coast Guard or other potential rescue agencies do not monitor grs bands.

(d) Bands tend to be crowded with undisciplined calling.

7.3.2 Amateur radio service (HAM RADIO)

In some circumstances, such as long distance ocean voyaging, *Amateur Radio* may be of interest to boaters.

It is possible to communicate over very great distances by the use of *Ham Radio*. There is seldom a time when someone can not be reached, and messages may be transmitted around the world through the worldwide network of amateurs.

VHF operation, particularly 2 metres (144 MHz) is quite popular among boating "hams". Amateur VHF equipment is similar in size and power requirements to marine VHF. A basic Amateur licence allows operation on VHF, and can be obtained without knowledge of Morse Code.

Just as with GRS, there are some drawbacks to the use of MF/HF Amateur Radio:

(a) Equipment can have large power requirements and tends to be expensive.

(b) Acquisition of an operator's certificate is relatively difficult compared to obtaining a ROC(M).

(c) No emergency assistance agencies monitor these frequencies.

7.3.3 Family Radio Service (FRS)

This is a UHF service (460 MHz) intended for short range communication—typically under 1 km. No licence is required. May be used for on-board communications. No emergency assistance agencies monitor this frequency.

7.3.4 General Mobile Radio Service (GMRS)

This is a unlicenced personal radio service. GMRS radios are higher power than FRS, and claim a range of eight miles. GMRS and FRS share seven channels. Each service has several channels not used by the other service.

Note; as the FRS/GMRS services in Canada and the United States operate on the same frequencies, our FRS/ GMRS radios can be used in the United States. However, other countries have similar services that operate on different frequencies, so our radios should not be used outside Canada and the United States.

module 2

Maritime Radio Course

Module 2

Section 4.0

Introduction

This module is intended to be used either as a 'bridging' module for boaters already in possession of a Restricted Operator's Certificate ROC(M), or to be taught as the second module of the CPS Maritime Radio Course.

For this reason Section 1.0 has been designed to serve as a 'refresher' for those already in possession of an ROC(M), and as a review for those who have just completed Module 1 of the CPS Maritime Radio Course.

Successful completion of this module qualifies the boater for the dsc endorsement on the Restricted Operator's Certificate ROC(M).

It should be noted that as in Module 1 of the CPS Maritime Radio Course, this module provides only the general knowledge associated with DSC/GMDSS and the relevant equipment. Because of the many manufacturers now producing DSC/GMDSS equipment, and their various models, it does not go into the detailed operation of the equipment. Boaters are encouraged to study the equipment manufacturer's instruction manuals for detailed information concerning the operation of their specific equipment.

If you have any questions, do not hesitate to ask your instructor. He or she will be pleased to assist you. We hope you enjoy this DSC/GMDSS module!

module 2

Maritime
Radio Course
Student's Notes

Section 1

1.0 Traditional system

1.1 Regulations

1.1.1 General

Installation of GMDSS equipment on Pleasure craft is considered to be 'voluntary'. The only requirement for such installations is that VHF-DSC radios must have an assigned Maritime Mobile Service Identity (MMSI) number. These numbers are obtainable from Industry Canada free of charge. EPIRBs must be registered in the Canadian National Beacon Database. It must be remembered, however, that the previously applicable regulations must still be complied with.

1.1.2 Restricted Operator's Certificate ROC(M)

As in the past, while foreign vessels operating in Canada must be in compliance with the regulations of their own country, a Restricted Radio Operator's Certificate ROC(M) is required by the operator of a VHF marine radio on a voluntarily equipped Canadian vessel.

1.1.3 Radio station licence

Most pleasure craft with VHF radio installations will meet the 'station licence exemption requirements', and will not require a station licence if they are operating in Canadian waters, or waters of countries having a reciprocal agreement with Canada. The radios must, however, be operated only on the marine frequencies as established by Industry Canada. A station licence, if required, may be obtained from Industry Canada. Such licence is renewable annually for a fee.

1.1.4 Radio log

While not mandatory for voluntary equipped vessels, keeping a Radio Log is a good practice and is highly recommended, particularly with respect to emergency communications.

1.1.5 Secrecy

Radio communications are considered to be privileged information, and as such mariners are obligated by law not to divulge the contents or even the existence of communications received (other than Distress, Urgency or Safety messages) which were intended for someone else. The Radiocommunication Act and the Contraventions Act provide for severe penalties for offences.

1.1.6 Additional

Details on exemption requirements, frequencies, the Radiocommunication Act, Regulations, and a listing of Industry Canada offices may be found in the appendices at the back of this module.

1.2 Procedures

1.2.1 Uses

Marine radios may be used to transmit Distress, Urgency and Safety messages as well as to communicate with other vessels. It may *not* be used to make superfluous transmissions, cause interference, use profane or offensive language, nor transmit false distress messages.

1.2.2 Operation

Transmissions should be clear, concise, and made at a reasonable speed—neither too slow nor too quickly. Brevity will help reduce frequency congestion.

1.2.3 Phonetics

This is very important! The phonetic alphabet must be memorized and used whenever communications are difficult or whenever it is necessary to spell out words.

1.2.4 Words and phrases

As with phonetics, the standard marine/aviation phraseology should be learned and used. Do not use the 'CB' language as it does not sound professional and it does not use approved vocabulary and procedures in emergencies.

1.2.5 Time

The 24-hour clock should be used. In local waters use the local time. In international waters Universal Coordinated Time (UTC), previously known as Greenwich Mean Time, should be used.

1.2.6 Call signs

Vessels with a radio station licence will be assigned a *call sign.* If the vessel has a name, the vessel name usually precedes the vessel call sign (number assigned by Industry Canada). Vessels without an assigned call sign (i.e. without a station licence) should use their vessel name only. If a vessel has neither a vessel name nor a call sign, it is suggested that the operators substitute their own name for identification purposes.

1.2.7 Calling

Before transmitting on the calling channel, listen to ensure the frequency is not already in use, and particularly, that a distress situation is not in progress. The name of the vessel being called *always precedes* the name of the vessel making the call. If you get no response after two calls, wait at least three minutes or longer before calling again. The station being called will specify the working channel to change to. Again keep in mind the need for brevity.

1.2.8 Simplex

Communication is on a single frequency only—both transmitting and receiving. Only one station can transmit at one time, otherwise the channel is jammed.

1.2.9 Duplex

Some channels are designated for duplex operation. A duplex channel uses two frequencies—one for transmitting, the other for receiving. This enables both stations to transmit simultaneously (like a telephone conversation). The VHF radios commonly used on pleasure craft are not equipped for full duplex operation, so the normal push-to-talk type of operation is used on these channels, although a telephone company's station will operate in full duplex mode.

1.2.10 Radio checks

Do not use Channel 16. Obtain checks, if required, from Coast Guard or another station on a working channel.

1.2.11 Channels

Use the channels listed in Industry Canada's list of frequencies, and select for the purposes shown (see Appendix 1 - RBR-2 Schedule 1).

1.2.12 Priorities

Keep in mind that Distress, Urgency, and Safety, in that order are the top three priorities for radio use. Distress calls have priority over all other radio communications and all other vessels are to cease transmissions which may interfere with the distress communications. Vessels receiving a Distress call and in a position to render assistance are required to do so, and should advise the Coast Guard they are responding. If the Distress is not acknowledged and the vessel is not in a position to provide assistance, a Mayday Relay should be transmitted to the Coat Guard by the receiving statation.

Communication Channel 16 may not be resumed until such time as the Distress is cancelled.

Urgency communications are also carried out on Channel 16. They may be transmitted to a specific station or to all stations. The Safety call is initiated on Channel 16. The call should also advise of the working channel on which the detailed message may be received.

1.2.13 Other

The CPS Maritime Radio Course focuses primarily on marine VHF-FM for coastal inland water communications. For offshore operations Marine MF/HF radios provide additional range and are monitored by Canadian Coast Guard stations.

Similarly, Amateur (Ham) radios also provide long-range communication capabilities, and while not monitored by the Coast Guard, are monitored throughout the world by Ham operators. Family Radio Service (FRS), General Mobile Radio Service (GMRS) and General Radio Service (GRS or CB) radios, while limited in range and not monitored by Coast Guard, can be used for short-range communication between vessels. Cellular telephones may allow you to contact Coast Guard if you are within cellular coverage, however it is not a good substitute for a marine radio. Unlike a marine radio, nearby boaters who may be in a position to assist, will not be alerted to the distress.

The Restricted Operator's Certificate, Maritime (ROC(M)) entitles the holder to operate VHF-MF and single-side band (HF) marine radios on voluntarily equipped vessels.

1.3 Shortcomings

1.3.1 Coverage

Because of a lack of shore stations, the present non-gmdss system is often limited to being in radio contact only with other vessels, not shore stations. This can result in some significant gaps in coverage.

1.3.2 Watchkeeping

Use of Morse Code, and the requirement to maintain a continuous listening watch meant full time radio officers were required on large ocean going vessels. The use of DSC means that vessels are no longer dependant on mariners having to listen for distress calls. DSC radios can do the monitoring now, and alert the crew.

USCG terminated watchkeeping on 2182 kHz and DSC 2187.5 kHz on August 1st, 2013. Additionally, marine information and weather broadcasts transmitted by USCG on 2670 kHz were also terminated on that date. The Canadian CG continues to monitor these frequencies and to provide broadcast services on 2 MHz. It has no plans to discontinue this service.

1.3.3 Position

Position of a vessel is manually determined and often can be inaccurate. With the GPS receivers supplying position data to a DSC capable radio, accurate position data will now be included in the DSC Distress Alert message.

Maritime
Radio Course
Student's Notes

Section 2

module 2

2.0 Global Maritime Distress and Safety System (GMDSS)

2.1 System overview

The Global Maritime Distress and Safety System (GMDSS) is an international system employing advanced digital and satellite technology. Development of GMDSS was initiated in 1988 by the International Maritime Organization (IMO). This system is a significant improvement in maritime communications. Prior to this, deep sea vessels and shore stations monitored Morse Code on 500 kHz. Coastal and deep sea ships also monitored MF 2182 kHz, and more recently VHF Channel 16. The limitations of this equipment and facilities did not ensure a reliable, well coordinated response to maritime distress situations. GMDSS is designed to enhance ship-to-shore communications, and to provide rapid, automated distress alerting. These functions, together with positional information, will overcome many of the above mentioned deficiencies.

2.1.1 Carriage requirements

Carriage of specified gmdss equipment is **mandatory** for large cargo ships and passenger ships on international voyages or in the open sea, as well as for non-pleasure-craft of closed construction more than eight metres (26 fee) in length, non-pleasure craft carrying more than six passengers, and towing vessels. It is **voluntary** for recreational vessels. GMDSS will have significant impact on recreational boaters, and it is recommended that all boaters become familiar with the system and its features.

2.1.2 Distress frequency monitoring

To help with the transition to GMDSS, Canadian Coast Guard stations will continue to monitor VHF Channel 16 and MF frequency 2182 kHz for the foreseeable future. The GMDSS equipment on these stations will also be monitoring for digital data on VHF Channel 70 and MF 2187.5 kHz. However, compulsorily equipped vessels are no longer obligated to monitor channels VHF 16 and MF frequency 2182 kHz. The GMDSS equipment on these vessels will instead be monitoring for digital data on VHF Channel 70 and MF frequency 2187.5 kHz. This may present problems for non-GMDSS equipped recreational vessels attempting voice communications with compulsorily equipped GMDSS equipped vessels who are no longer monitoring the traditional voice channels and frequencies.

2.2 GMDSS basic concept

Through the introduction of new mandatory equipment carriage requirements for all non-pleasure craft and the addition of satellite and shore communication facilities, a system has been developed which should enable any compliant vessel to alert shore stations of a distress situation by at least two separate and independent means.

To achieve this goal, mandatory equipment carriage requirements for non-pleasure craft are considerably greater than for voluntarily equipped pleasure craft. The figure 2.1 depicts the concept as it pertains to pleasure craft.

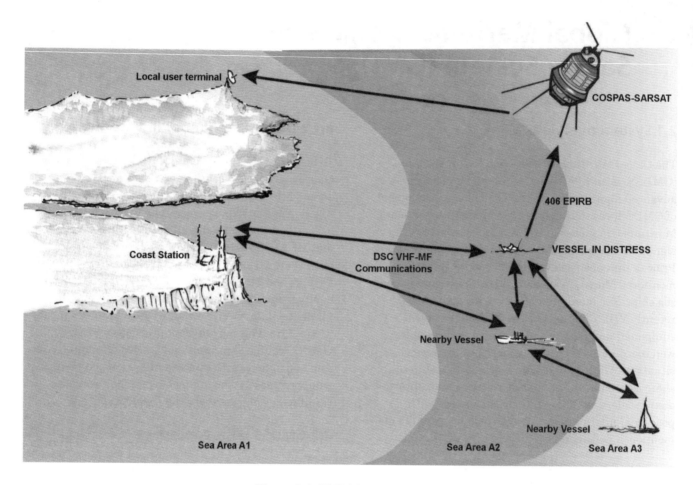

Figure 2.1: GMDSS basic concept

Maritime Radio Course
Student's Notes

Section 3

3.0 GMDSS regulations and application

3.1 Equipment requirements

3.1.1 International voyages

Since 1999/02/01, non-pleasure craft over 300 tons, and vessels carrying more than 12 passengers on international voyages were required to be fitted with gmdss equipment in accordance with the requirements of the Safety of Life at Sea (SOLAS) Convention. Generally speaking, depending on vessel length and the area which the ship is operating, such vessels are required to carry as a minimum, the following: a DSC radio installation, Search and Rescue Transponder (SART), portable VHF transceiver, NAVTEX receiver, inmarsat system, AIS and Emergency Position Indicating Radio Beacon (EPIRB).

3.1.2 Domestic non-pleasure craft

Since 2001/04/01, domestic non-pleasure craft over 300 tons and vessels 20 metres (66 feet) or more in length carrying more than 12 passengers are required to carry VHF-DSC equipment. Since 2003/08/01, vessels of closed construction more than eight metres (26 feet) in length, vessels carrying more than six passengers, and towing vessels are also required to carry VHF-DSC equipment.

3.1.3 Pleasure craft

Pleasure craft have no mandatory GMDSS equipment carriage requirements. Pleasure craft are considered voluntary vessels insofar as GMDSS equipment carriage requirements are concerned.

It is recommended however, that boaters holding an older Restricted Radio Certificate, complete Module 2 of the CPS Maritime Radio Course and obtain a DSC Endorsement for their Certificate.

3.1.4 Shore Stations

While carriage requirements for the various classes of vessels were mandated some time ago, it was obvious that for full operational capability, the shore stations would also have to have the required equipment. As this equipment was installed, areas were declared "operational". The east and west coasts of Canada and the U.S are now fully operational, as is the Great Lakes area.

3.2 Sea areas

The four sea areas

GMDSS divides the world's oceans into four "sea areas", designated A1 through A4. These areas were established to dictate the GMDSS equipment carriage requirements of compulsory equipped vessels.

3.2.1 Sea Area A1

This area falls within range of at least one shore-based VHF-DSC coast station (typically 20 nm from shore).

3.2.2 Sea Area A2

This falls within range of at least one shore-based MF-DSC coast station (typically 100 nm from shore, excluding Sea Area A1).

As of January 1st, 2014, neither the United States nor Canada has officially declared GMDSS Sea Area 2 officially operational.

3.2.3 Sea Area A3

This is within inmarsat satellite coverage, between 70°N and 70°S, excluding Sea Areas A1 and A2.

3.2.4 Sea Area A4

This includes the Polar Regions, excluding Sea Areas A1, A2 and A3.

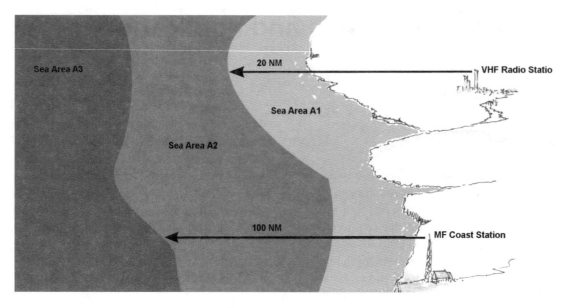

Figure 3.1: Sea Areas

3.2.5 Operations

While much of the world is still in either Sea Area A3 or Sea Area A4, most recreational vessels are operating in Sea Area A1 or A2. With the declaration of shore stations as operational, recreational vessels equipped with VHF-DSC radios should be able to make use of the GMDSS system, particularly in Sea Area A1. To date there has been little interest by either Canada or the U.S. in making Sea Area A2 officially operational.

3.2.6 Equipment requirements

The mandatory equipped vessels have increasingly stringent equipment carriage requirements as they transit from Sea Areas A1 through A4. Most recreational vessels, operating in Sea Areas A1 and A2, who wish to participate on a voluntary basis, will be equipped with a Digital Selective Calling (DSC) capable radio suitable to its normal operating area. It is also desirable to have a 406 MHz Emergency Position Indicating Radio Beacon (EPIRB). Ideally, compatible navigational positioning equipment such as GPS is also highly desirable. When interfaced with the DSC radio, GPS provides vessel position information automatically—an obvious valuable safety feature.

3.3 Maritime Mobile Service Identity (MMSI)

3.3.1 Vessel identification

Please note that DSC equipped vessels and shore stations are each assigned a unique identity number, known as a Maritime Mobile Service Identity (MMSI) number. This MMSI is exclusive to that specific vessel or station, and is not transferable. The MMSI consists of nine digits, the first three identify the country of origin. Canadian vessels are assigned 316, the continental United States numbers are 303, 338, 366, 367, 368 or 369. "Fleet" vessels from organizations such as yacht clubs or Canadian Power and Sail Squadrons may also obtain a unique fleet MMSI. They have one 0, and coast stations have two 0's preceding the country identifier.

Example: MMSI numbers
Typical Canadian Vessels 316123456
Fleet Vessels 031612345
Coast Guard 003161234

As a result, the existence of, or lack of, zeros in the first three digits of an MMSI number indicates the type of station (Fleet, Coast Guard or regular vessel). The country identifier will be the first three digits which are not zeros.

3.3.2 DSC MMSI prerequisite

It is absolutely essential that all vessels with DSC fixed mount radios obtain an MMSI number, and have it programmed into the radio. This is necessary because DSC transmit functions will not work until an MMSI number is entered. The same MMSI number is used on all radios on board the vessel. MMSI numbers are currently available from Industry Canada at no cost. Many of the new hand-held VHF radios now also incorporate DSC and in some cases GPS.

3.3.3 Industry Canada

Contact Industry Canada at their District Offices as listed in Appendix 7, or via the website – http://sd.ic.gc.ca to obtain an MMSI.

3.3.4 Routine calls

MMSI numbers are used in much the same way as telephone numbers. You make a routine call to another vessel by entering that vessel's MMSI number in your radio the same way as you make a cell phone call by entering the other person's phone number into your cell phone.

Only the initial call is handled digitally. Voice communication will take place on regular voice channels.

More details on making routine calls will be found in section 4.4.7 in Module 2 of this manual.

3.3.5 Ease of communication

With appropriate DSC equipment there is no longer a need to establish routine contact with another vessel on the usually very busy Calling/Distress voice channel VHF Channel 16, or MF frequency 2182 kHz. DSC equipped vessels will contribute significantly to reliability and ease of establishing communication, as well as reducing the present congestion on these channels.

3.4 Maritime Identity (MI)

The MI is used to identify other maritime devices, such as hand-held VHF-DSC radios not associated with a specific vessel; AIS search and rescue transmitters (AIS-SARTS); man overboard (MOB) devices; and emergency position-indicating beacons that use AIS technology (EPIRB-AIS).

In cases where the hand-held VHF-DSC radio is NOT associated with a specific ship station or vessel, Industry Canada may now issue a Maritime Identity (MI) registration for the hand-held VHF-DSC transceiver, rather than an MMSI. The MI also has nine digits, with the number 8 preceding the three country of origin numbers (i.e. 8316). Rationale is that the MI number might be useful to rescue agencies in an emergency, as these radios usually have a limited battery capacity and a restricted coverage area.

Maritime
Radio Course
Student's Notes

module 2

Section 4

4.0 Digital Selective Calling (DSC) radios

4.1 GMDSS primary component

The Digital Selective Calling (DSC) radio will be the primary component of gmdss used by recreational boaters.

4.1.1 Range limitation

VHF-DSC radios use the same VHF band as older VHF radios, so they have the same line of sight range. They do not use satellite technology other than for position via interface to units such as a GPS. This limitation must be recognized..

4.1.2 Large non-pleasure craft

Non-pleasure craft over 300 tons, and vessels carrying more than 12 passengers on international voyages are required to be fitted with GMDSS equipment including DSC radio equipment. Similarly, domestic vessels over 300 tons and vessels 20 m (66 ft) or more in length, carrying more than 12 passengers on domestic voyages are required to carry VHF-DSC equipment.

4.1.3 Smaller non-pleasure craft

Non-pleasure craft of closed construction more than 8 metres (26 ft.) in length, non-pleasure craft carrying more than 6 passengers, and towing vessels are required to carry VHF-DSC equipment.

4.1.4 DSC radio standards

New VHF-DSC radios manufactured for commercial carriage requirements were initially quite expensive. To encourage manufacturers to produce VHF-DSC radios for the recreational market, the United States Federal Communications Commission (FCC) and Industry Canada, approved VHF-DSC radios to be built to a less stringent technical standard. This standard was referred to as the SC-101 Standard. Radios built to this standard did not have all the features of radios built to compulsorily fitted vessels, which required as

a minimum radios built to the more stringent Class D Standard.

SC-101 radios only had one receiver, so if the VHF-DSC radio was already engaged in a voice call, the DSC signal coming in on the DSC channel 70, would be missed. Class D radios with their two receivers of course did not have this problem. As well the SC-101 radios lacked many other desirable features found in Class D radios.

As the cost of Class D Standard radios came down, The FCC discontinued the SC-101 Standard, and Industry Canada ceased approval of SC-101 class radios.

4.1.5 DSC radio selection

Since the U.S. no longer permits the sale of SC-101 radios, and Industry Canada no longer approves SC-101 radios, Class D VHF-DSC radios are now considered the standard for recreational boaters.

Some newer VHF-DSC radios now incorporate Global Positioning System (GPS) receivers, Automatic Identification System (AIS) receivers, and other useful functions at little or no extra cost.

Figure 4.1: VHF-DSC radio with Distress button

4.1.6 Channel 70 use

Channel 70 is designated exclusively for DSC digital use, and is monitored automatically by VHF-DSC radios. DSC-capable radios will not allow voice transmissions on Channel 70.

4.1.7 Routine calling

In addition to the distress-alerting feature, the DSC system also permits originating routine calls to other vessels. To do this, the MMSI of the other vessel is either entered manually, or selected from previously-entered numbers in the radio's "phone book", and a desired working channel is selected. The radio will then send a digital signal on channel 70 which will cause the other vessel's radio to sound a routine call "alert" signal. When the other vessel acknowledges the call, both radios will automatically switch to the selected working channel, and voice communication can commence. (Only the initial call "alert" is sent digitally on Ch 70. The resulting voice communications will occur on the regular voice working channel.)

4.1.8 Position information

Position information obtained from an interfaced gps receiver, or manually input, is included in the digital Distress message sent on Channel 70. This position information can be requested by other DSC equipped vessels by sending a position request or polling message.

4.1.9 Alert

An audible 'alert' signal is provided to the operator by the DSC radio upon receipt of an incoming signal. The "alert" signal for a distress alert is distinctly different (and more urgent sounding) than that for other calls.

4.1.10 DSC radio identification

DSC radios are readily identifiable by the distinctive, dedicated red button marked 'Distress' which has a protective lid or cover to prevent accidental activation.

4.2 Classes of DSC radios

In order to meet the International Maritime Organization (IMO) GMDSS carriage requirements for different vessels, a number of DSC radio standards, or 'classes' were defined. Carriage requirements were determined according to the type of vessel, and the area of operation.

4.2.1 Class A

This class fulfils all IMO GMDSS requirements for MF/HF radios on compulsorily fitted vessels over 300 GRT.

4.2.2 Class B

This class fulfils minimum imo gmdss requirements for MF and VHF radios on non-pleasure craft not required to carry Class A equipment.

4.2.3 Class C

This class has been withdrawn and is not approved for use.

4.2.4 Class D

This fulfils the minimum requirements for VHF-DSC radios on non-pleasure craft not required to carry Class A or Class B equipment. It should be noted that not all Class D radios necessarily meet imo gmdss compulsory carriage requirements.

4.2.5 SC-101

The U.S. no longer permits the sale of SC-101 radios, and Industry Canada no longer approves SC-101 radios. Class D VHF-DSC radios are now considered the standard for recreational boaters.

4.2.6 Class E

This class is similar to Class D but for MF/HF equipment.

4.3 DSC functions

4.3.1 DSC features

It should be understood that DSC features will speed initializing contact with other stations, but DSC is NOT used for voice communication. DSC alerts the called station digitally on Channel 70 and then both stations move to a working channel. No voice communication is transmitted on Channel 70.

As time goes by, and more and more people use DSC, the congestion on Channel 16 will be relieved. The integration of GPS with a DSC radio greatly increases position reporting accuracy. Features such as polling will help you make contact with unknown stations. Many low cost radios have an impressive list of features.

4.3.2 DSC functions

All DSC radios will automatically send a Distress call and message at the press of a special designated 'DISTRESS' button to coast stations and other DSC equipped vessels in the immediate area. At this time, not all radios have DSC, so mariners should follow up their DSC transmission with the usual voice MAYDAY call and message on VHF Channel 16.

This button is usually red in colour, marked 'Distress', and has a cover to avoid accidental activation. To further enhance safety, unless the radio has an integrated GPS, interfacing a GPS with the DSC radio is highly recommended in order to ensure that the vessel's position is transmitted. If an interface is not possible, the operator is required to input a position manually at frequent intervals (minimum of every 4 hours). The automated Distress message provides information as to the identity of the vessel, the nature of the distress (some radios), and location of the vessel. It also sounds an alarm at other DSC equipped stations. Boaters should attempt contact with the vessel in distress on Channel 16 (see section 4.3.2.1), relay the distress if necessary, and make sure the shore station is made aware of the distress. Follow-up voice communications on VHF Channel 16 or a working channel would be assigned by the shore station and then carried out as in the past.

4.3.2.1 Terminating the DSC Distress Call

A DSC Distress call is automatically repeated over and over at intervals until digitally answered by another ship or turned off by the operator. Usually, the Coast Guard provides a DSC reply and that signal automatically turns off the DSC Distress call. It is not desirable for just any responding vessel to turn off the Distress vessel's distress signal, and so

SC-101 and Class D radios are not equipped to digitally acknowledge a distress.

If the Coast Guard does not acknowledge the distress, you should do so verbally on Channel 16 and then try to contact the Coast Guard to advise them of the situation.

Some radios on commercial vessels have the ability to turn off a distress vessel's DSC Distress call by responding digitally, but they should not do so unless they are advised to by the Coast Guard or a Rescue Coordination Center (RCC).

4.3.3 Watchkeeping

The DSC radio automatically, silently, and continuously maintains a listening watch on the appropriate DSC channel, VHF Channel 70.

Note: With some of the less expensive DSC radios (SC-101) which do not have two independent receivers incorporated, the continuous monitoring of Channel 70 may be interrupted when the radio is in the process of transmitting or receiving on another channel.

USCG terminated watchkeeping on 2182 kHz and DSC 2187.5 kHz on August 1st, 2013. Additionally, marine information and weather broadcasts transmitted on 2670 kHz by USCG were also terminated on that date. The Canadian CG continues to monitor 2182 kHz and provide broadcast services on 2 MHz, and has no plans to discontinue this service.

4.3.4 Capabilities

As stated earlier, DSC capabilities are not limited to emergencies. All Ships, Urgency and Safety alerts may also be received and sent to or from coast stations, and all DSC equipped vessels in the immediate area. The actual Urgency and Safety messages are subsequently carried out as in the past by normal voice communications on the channels/frequencies indicated in the DSC Alert.

4.3.5 Initial contact

Another extremely important and useful feature is that vessels with DSC radios are able to establish initial contact for routine calls with other DSC equipped vessels through use of the mmsi. By entering the mmsi number, a digital message is transmitted, sounding an alert on the vessel being called. A message is displayed on the front of the radio advising the vessel of the specific channel/frequency on which voice communications are to be carried out. Upon acknowledgement (digitally), both vessels change to the specified working channel for voice communications. It should be noted that some DSC radios will automatically change to the desired voice communication channel. This discreet routine call feature will not only provide improved reliability and ease of operation, but more importantly, it should significantly reduce the congestion on Channel 16.

4.3.6 Summary

Summarizing, the DSC radio enables vessels to rapidly transmit a Distress alert and message, digitally alert other vessels that an Urgency or Safety message is about to be sent, receive Distress, Urgency and Safety alerts, and to establish routine contact with other vessels and coast stations directly, without having to use the voice calling/distress channels.

4.4 DSC procedures

4.4.1 Operational procedures

Due to the differences between DSC radios from different manufacturers, it is not possible to describe each operational procedure specifically. Procedures described herein are of a general nature only. Boaters should become thoroughly familiar with the manual provided by the manufacturer of their specific radio.

4.4.2 DSC optimization

As stated in section 3.3.2, DSC functions will not work unless the radio has an MMSI number programmed into it. This may be done by the dealer or in many cases the operator. Radios programmable by the operator may allow only a limited number of attempts (e.g.,

three tries). In addition to the MMSI number, it is highly desirable to have a GPS connected to the DSC radio. If no navigational equipment is interfaced, the vessel's position must be input manually on a regular basis (minimum of every 4 hours).

4.4.3 Distress procedure

In a distress situation, time permitting, if the radio is not connected to a navigational device, the boat operator must manually input the vessel's position (latitude and longitude) and time, select the type of distress from the menu if one is provided, lift the red cover and depress the 'Distress' button for 5 seconds. (or until the display changes to acknowledgment mode). The DSC radio will transmit the Distress call on Channel 70 automatically every 3.5 minutes to 4.5 minutes, until a digital acknowledgement is received or the distress is cancelled.

As previously stated, there is no voice communication on Channel 70. Also, one must realize that not all vessels are equipped with DSC. Therefore once the distress call is issued on Channel 70 by pressing the red distress button, you should change to Channel 16 and issue a verbal Mayday call. Some radios will automatically switch to Channel 16 after using the distress button. See your user's manual for full details.

4.4.4 Distress response

When the digital acknowledgement is received, reply on Channel 16. Other vessels should not acknowledge receipt of a DSC Distress alert via DSC unless requested to do so by a coast station or an RCC. Doing so would terminate transmission of the DSC Distress message by the vessel in distress. Normally acknowledgement is expected to be made by the coast station. Boaters should attempt contact with the vessel in distress on **Channel 16,** relay the distress if necessary, and make sure the shore station is made aware of the distress. Ensure the distress is cancelled when the situation is concluded.

4.4.5 Urgency procedure

The Urgency signal indicates that a station has a very urgent message to transmit concerning the safety of a ship, aircraft or other vehicle or the safety of a person. To transmit a DSC Urgency alert, select the 'All Ships' function. Specify the working channel as 16 unless the message is very lengthy, in which case specify another working channel, such as 06. The Urgency alert will be transmitted on Channel 70. After a brief wait to allow the other vessels to change to Channel 16, broadcast your urgency message using standard VHF procedures preceded by the PAN PAN, PAN PAN, PAN PAN prefix. As in a Distress situation, the Urgency requires cancellation when concluded.

4.4.6 Safety procedure

The Safety signal indicates that a station has an important message to transmit concerning an important navigational aid or a meteorological warning. To transmit a DSC Safety alert, you may select the All Ships function and specify a working channel other than 16, such as 06. The Safety alert will be transmitted on Channel 70. After a brief wait to allow the other vessels to change to the specified channel, broadcast your safety message using standard VHF procedures, preceded as usual by the SECURITE', SECURITE', SECURITE' prefix.

However, rather than using the DSC procedure, and in order to avoid unnecessary loading of the distress and safety calling frequencies specified for use with digital selective calling techniques, the following technique is now recommended for the transmission of safety messages:

– *safety messages which only concern vessels in the vicinity should **not** be announced by digital selective calling techniques, rather by using standard non-digital selective calling procedures as outlined in Module 1 – Section 5.*

4.4.7 Routine call procedure

Routine individual calls to Routine individual calls to other DSC equipped vessels or coast stations are relatively straightforward. Before a caller can contact another station it is essential that, just as with a pager or telephone, he/she must use the number (MMSI) of the station being called. On many DSC radios a memory or directory is available to store the name and MMSI of frequently called numbers.

The caller selects the channel on which the voice communications are to be carried out. Note, this is contrary to the concept of 'control' which was discussed in Module One. In traditional communications it is the called station that has control and selects the working channel. With DSC, you select the MMSI number of the station you are calling, and then transmit the message digitally on Channel 70. The other vessel will receive an audible alert (usually different from the Distress alert) indicating the caller's MMSI and the proposed channel on which voice communication is desired. When acknowledged, some radios will automatically change to the voice channel pre-selected for communication, and voice communication can begin, without having to use Channel 16.

4.4.8 Repeating a routine call

If an acknowledgement is not received within 5 minutes of attempting a routine call, the call may be repeated. Further repeat attempts should not be made for at least 15 minutes. The DSC call will trigger an audible tone at the called DSC radio if it is turned ON. If an acknowledgement is not received, it may be that the called station is not turned ON, or the operator is not available to answer the call. If ON, most DSC radios will log and display a message indicating a call had been received and an acknowledgement is requested. Some DSC radios also have a built in 5 minute delay before a second attempt may be repeated.

4.4.9 Testing a DSC radio's Distress button

How can you test your radio to see if the Distress button works properly? We have asked this question of Industry Canada. The official answer is "You can't". You cannot legally test the Distress function. It is to be assumed that if you can make a routine call, your equipment can make a Distress call.

Maritime
Radio Course
Student's Notes

Section 5

5.0 Emergency Position Indicating Radio Beacons (EPIRBs)

5.1 EPIRBs

Another very useful piece of GMDSS equipment for recreational boaters when some distance from shore, is the 406 MHz Emergency Position Indicating Radio Beacon, or EPIRB. These buoyant beacons operate on the international distress frequency 406 MHz, and when activated automatically transmit a distress message digitally to orbiting COSPAS–SARSAT satellites, and a NOAAgeostationary satellite system.

Figure 5.1: 406 MHz EPIRB

5.1.1 Category 1 EPIRB

This may be activated manually or automatically. The automatic activation is usually triggered after the EPIRB is released from a specially designed bracket. The bracket is equipped with a hydrostatic device that releases the EPIRB at a water depth of l metre to 3 metres (3 feet to 10 feet), and the EPIRB then floats to the surface and begins transmitting. A Category 1

EPIRB must be mounted externally where it will be able to readily float free from a sinking vessel.

5.1.2 Category 2 EPIRB

This requires manual activation and does not float free automatically. It should be mounted in a location readily accessible in an emergency situation.

5.1.3 Locating

Most 406 MHz EPIRBs have a strobe light. This light assists rescue vessels in locating the EPIRB and indicates visually that the EPIRB is transmitting. Many 406 MHz EPIRBs include a low powered 121.5 MHz signal for homing. The homing signal may be picked up by a SAR vessel or aircraft.

5.1.4 Positional Accuracy

EPIRBs may or may not incorporate a GPS. If the EPIRB does not incorporate a GPS, the satellites can determine the EPIRB's position to within 5 Km. With a GPS, the position accuracy can be within 125 metres or less. It is strongly recommended that you purchase an EPIRB with a built-in GPS as these units will ensure a much quicker and more accurate response from Search and Rescue.

5.1.5 Tests

Both Category 1 and 2 epirbs have built in test functions. Make sure to refer to the manufacturers' instructions for testing them. Batteries should be replaced on or before the expiration date.

5.1.6 Registration

EPIRBs must be registered in a national database, in Canada, the Canadian Beacon Registry (Tel. 1-877-406-7671) www.canadianbeaconregistry.forces.gc.ca, or in the U.S.A., the Sarsat Beacon Registry, National

Oceanographic and Atmospheric Administration (NOAA), Suitland , MD (Tel. 1888-212-7283) www.sarsat.noaa.gov.

5.1.7 EPIRB identity

This satellite system relies on the EPIRB number for identification, so it is essential that the EPIRB be properly registered with the appropriate authorities, and that these authorities are also advised if the EPIRB changes ownership.

5.2 COSPAS–SARSAT satellite system

This is an international system consisting of two orbiting satellite systems designed to detect EPIRB 406 MHz distress signals. It was established jointly by Russia, France, Canada and the U.S.A. for the purpose of monitoring distress signals from EPIRBs.

GPS CONSTELLATION OF SATELLITES

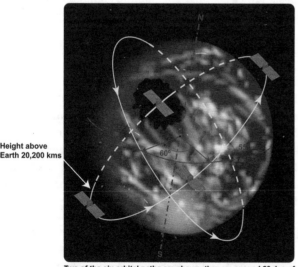

Height above
Earth 20,200 kms

Two of the six orbital paths are shown, they are spaced 60 deg of longitude apart.   Only the four GPS satellites in one orbit, 90 deg apart, are shown

Figure 5.2: COSPAS–SARSAT satellite system

5.2.1 Orbit

The COSPAS satellites orbit at 1000 kilometres (621 miles) and are controlled by Russia. The SARSAT satellites orbit at 850 kilometres (528 miles) and are controlled by the U.S.A. At any given time a minimum of four satellites are operational. Orbit time is approximately 100 minutes.

5.2.2 Response time

The time for response may be as little as 30 minutes; however it could be as long as up to 2 hours depending on EPIRB/satellite relative positions.

5.2.3 Coverage

The COSPAS-SARSAT system provides worldwide coverage, and position is determined using the Doppler shift principle. Doppler shift is a measure of the change in relative motion between the satellite and the EPIRB, to determine the position of the EPIRB.

5.2.4 Registration

Provided the EPIRB has been properly registered, Search and Rescue personnel will be able to readily identify the owner of the EPIRB transmitting the distress from its existing database, and dispatch rescue vessels and aircraft.

Maritime
Radio Course
Student's Notes

module 2

Section 6

6.0 Other GMDSS equipment

6.1 MF/HF DSC radios

6.1.1 Requirement

MF DSC radios are required for DSC operations at distances beyond Sea Area A1, but within Sea Area A2. Boaters contemplating voyages beyond VHF coverage should consider installation of an MF DSC radio.

Radios covering only the MF band (2 MHz) are no longer available. Current radios covering this band will also cover the HF band.

Figure 6.1: MF/HF Radio

6.1.2 Digital calling

The frequency 2187.5 kHz is the MF designated DSC frequency.

USCG terminated watchkeeping on 2182 kHz and DSC 2187.5 kHz on August 1st, 2013. Additionally, marine information and weather broadcasts 2670 kHz by USCG were also terminated on that date. The Canadian CG however continues to monitor 2182 kHz and DSC 2187.5 kHz, and to provide broadcast services on 2 MHz. It has no plans to discontinue this service.

6.1.3 Voice calling

The frequency 2182 kHz is the MF frequency for voice communications.

6.2 Portable VHF radios

6.2.1 Requirements

Many non-pleasure craft are required by regulation to carry one or more portable VHF radios. Primarily they are intended on these vessels for emergency use on lifeboats.

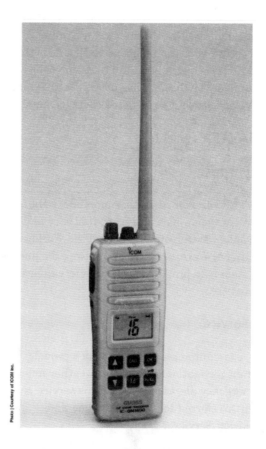

Figure 6.2: portable VHF Radio

6.2.2 Uses

A portable VHF radio is useful on pleasure craft as a back up to the fixed VHF radio, as it is not dependent on the vessel's batteries or antenna installation.

6.2.3 Limitations

Other than on very small vessels where it is impractical to fit a fixed VHF radio, a portable VHF radio should not be considered as a substitute for a fixed radio, due to its relatively low power output, small antenna and limited battery life.

6.2.4 Maritime Identity (MI)

In cases where the hand-held VHF-DSC radio is <u>NOT</u> associated with a specific ship station or vessel, Industry Canada may now issue a Maritime Identity (MI) registration for the hand-held VHF-DSC transceiver, rather than an MMSI. The MI also has nine digits, with the number 8 preceding the three country of origin numbers. Rationale is that the MI number might be useful to rescue agencies in an emergency, as these radios usually have a limited battery capacity and a restricted coverage area.

6.3 NAVTEX receivers

6.3.1 Purpose

A NAVTEX receiver is another mandatory equipment item on many non-pleasure craft. It is very important from a safety standpoint. As part of the Worldwide Navigational Warning Service (wwnws), the purpose of this system is to provide maritime safety information to vessels at sea.

6.3.2 Service

navtex is an automated system, which provides important navigational warnings, weather information, and emergency alerts to vessels. This service is frequently referred to as the Maritime Safety Information Service.

6.3.3 Data

The relevant data is provided for transmission by Hydrographic offices, Meteorological offices, Rescue Coordination Centres, and International Ice Patrol.

6.3.4 Areas

To ensure worldwide coverage, the navtex system is made up of 16 'Nav' areas, each of which can have up to 24 transmitting stations. Each station has an assigned identification letter.

6.3.5 Frequency

Operating on a receiving frequency of 518 kHz, the information is provided on either a display unit and/or printed out by a printer.

6.4 Search and Rescue Transponders (SARTs)

Figure 6.3: Search and Rescue Transponder

6.4.1 Purpose

The purpose of the Search and Rescue Transponder is to assist in locating vessels in distress and survivors. It is a small portable device that can be fitted to the life raft, or easily taken aboard the life raft when abandoning ship becomes necessary.

6.4.2 Locating

When interrogated* by a rescue vessel's X band 9 GHz
radar, or a similar airborne radar, the SART responds
with a signal generating 12 blips on the searcher's
radar. These blips extend outward from the SART's
position along its line of bearing (see figure 6.4).

6.4.3 Response

The SART will indicate being interrogated by emitting
an aural tone and a flashing light. If interrogation
ceases for more than 15 seconds, the SART reverts back
to the 'Standby' mode to conserve battery power.

6.4.4 Accuracy

As the rescue craft approaches the vessel with the
SART, the 12 blips change into wide arcs. Next the arcs
become complete circles, when the distance decreases to
below one mile. This alerts the rescue craft to the close
proximity of the SART.

6.4.5 Usefulness

The SART response is quite distinctive and is actually
a transmitter. It is much more effective than a radar
reflector.

---

* Interrogation — A radar signal from a vessel or aircraft
  is sent out to the SART. This is considered to be
  'interrogating' the SART.

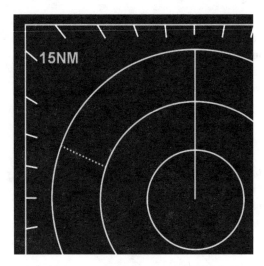

Radar display showing the SART 12 dot
blip code (bearing approximately 30 degrees to port)

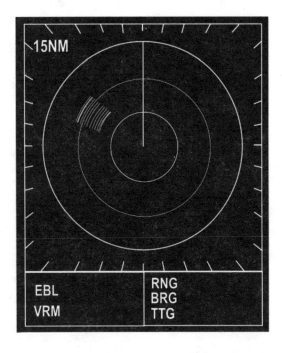

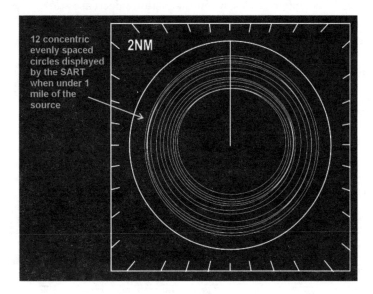

As the search craft approaches to within
about 10 nautical miles of the SART, the 12 dots will
change to wide arcs, then into complete
circles as the rescue vessel gets within 1 mile.

Figure 6.4: Activated Search and Rescue Transponder on radar

2

Maritime
Radio Course
Student's Notes

Section 7

7.0 DSC practical exercises (optional–recommended)

Students will demonstrate on actual equipment, or if equipment is not available, provide an explanation of Distress, Urgency, Safety, and Routine calls. The sequences and operation of VHF-DSC radios shown below are examples of these calls. VHF-DSC radios from different manufacturers, while similar, will likely vary somewhat. Reference to the owner's manual is recommended.

7.1 Distress call

a) Determine that grave and imminent danger threatens a vessel or person and immediate assistance is required.

b) If time permits, select nature of distress.

c) Lift protective cover and press red distress button for five seconds.

d) Make a voice distress call on Channel 16. (MAYDAY)

e) Monitor Channel 16.

7.2 Urgency call (all ships)

a) Determine that it is an Urgency situation–safety of a vessel or person.

b) Select "All Ships", then "Urgency" from the menu (or as specified in your owner's manual)

c) Select Channel 16 as default channel.

d) Press enter key

e) Wait briefly for other vessels to switch to Channel 16.

f) On Channel 16, transmit
PAN PAN PAN PAN PAN PAN
ALL STATIONS ALL STATIONS ALL STATIONS
This is (the vessel call sign or MMSI) followed by the urgent message.

7.3 Safety call (all ships)

a) Determine that it is a Safety situation—important message concerning navigation or meteorological warning.

b) Select "All Ships", then "Safety" from the menu (or as specified in the owner's manual).

c) Select Channel 06 as default channel.

d) Press Enter key

e) Wait briefly for other vessels to switch to Channel 06.

f) On Channel 06, transmit
SECURITÉ SECURITÉ SECURITÉ
ALL STATIONS ALL STATIONS ALL STATIONS
This is (the vessel call sign or MMSI) followed by the safety message.

Note: To avoid unnecessary loading of the distress and safety calling frequencies specified for use with digital selective calling techniques, safety messages After *which only concern vessels in the vicinity should <u>not</u> be announced by digital selective calling techniques, <u>rather by using standard non-digital selective calling procedures as outlined in Module 1 – Section 5.</u>*

7.4 Routine call (to another vessel)

a) Enter the MMSI or select a station from the directory.

b) Select the desired working channel.

c) Press enter key.

7.5 Acknowledging calls (distress, all ships, routine)

7.5.1 Distress

Mute the alarm. Note the mmsi, position, time, and nature of distress.

If a Coast Station does not acknowledge the distress call within 2 minutes and if you are in a position to assist, attempt to contact the vessel in distress on Channel 16.

If a Coast Station has not acknowledged, attempt to contact the coast station on Channel 16 as well.

Even if your radio has the ability to digitally acknowledge a call, do not attempt to acknowledge the distress digitally via dsc, as this will cancel the distress transmissions.

7.5.2 All ships

Mute the alarm and respond to receipt of an All Ships alert by switching to the channel specified by the station which initiated the All Ships call.

7.5.3 Routine

Mute the alarm, and an acknowledgement will be sent digitally to the station initiating the call. If the radio has not automatically changed to the requested working channel, do so manually and proceed with the call.

GMDSS review questions (25)

1. What is the one very important additional requirement when a VHF-DSC radio is installed replacing a non-DSC radio?

    _____

2. Does the operator of a pleasure craft have to acquire a ROC(M) if the radio is a VHF without DSC and is operated only in Canada?

    _____

3. Are all pleasure craft exempt from having to have a Radio Station Licence?

    _____

4. Under what circumstances is it recommended that a Radio Log be kept?

    _____

5. Which government acts are used in the enforcement of radio regulation?

    _____

6. What are three types of radio transmissions that are not permitted?

    _____

7. When should phonetics be used?

    _____

8. Who assigns radio call signs? When are they assigned?

    _____

9. When should the 24-hour clock be used?

    _____

10. How long should you wait before attempting to call again if no response has been received after two calls?

    _____

11. How do you determine which particular radio frequency should be used?

_____

12. What are the three priority calls that take precedence over all other radio transmissions?

_____

13. What was one of the shortcomings of the non-DSC, VHF communications system?

_____

14. Give two advantages of GMDSS.

_____

15. Which vhf channel is used for the transmission of digital information?

_____

16. How far from shore does Sea Area A1 extend?

_____

17. What is meant by the term MMSI?

_____

18. Is it mandatory to have an MMSI before operating the VHF-DSC radio using Channel 70?

_____

19. How would you obtain a fleet MMSI for use by your Squadron?

_____

20. When may VHF-DSC radios of the SC-101 specification be installed on compulsorily fitted vessels?

_____

21. How is a vessel with a VHF-DSC radio 'alerted' to an incoming call?

_____

22. How is the accidental activation of the Distress button prevented?

_____

23. Why is it important for a vessel to wait for the Coast Guard to acknowledge a DSC distress alert?

_____

_____

24. If the VHF-DSC radio is not interfaced with a GPS how frequently must position data be input to the VHF-DSC radio?

_____

25. Name two types of electronic safety equipment other than VHF-DSC radio or GPS, that a pleasure boater should consider for a voyage offshore?

_____

_____

Answers to GMDSS review questions (25)

1. An MMSI number must be obtained from Industry Canada and programmed into the VHF-DSC radio.

2. Yes. All persons operating a radio in the Maritime Mobile Service in Canadian waters are required to have a Restricted Operators Certificate (Maritime). (Persons on foreign vessels must be in compliance with the regulations of that country).

3. No. Only if they meet the 'station license exemption requirements'.

4. It is good practice at all times, but particularly with respect to emergency communications.

5. Radiocommunications Act and Contraventions Act.

6. False Distress, Profane and Offensive language, and Interference/Superfluous transmissions.

7. When pronouncing isolated letters or groups of letters separately, or when communication is difficult.

8. Industry Canada when a radio station license is issued.

9. Whenever time is expressed in the Maritime Mobile Service.

10. At least three minutes or longer.

11. Refer to RBR-2 Radio Aids to Marine Navigation, or from information obtained from Industry Canada District or Regional Offices. (see Appendix 1)

12. Distress, Urgency, Safety.

13. Inadequate coverage, full time watch keeping requirements, inaccurate position information.

14. Enhanced ship to shore communications, automated distress calling, more accurate position information, more discreet routine calling.

15. Channel 70.

16. Typically 20 nautical miles.

17. Maritime Mobile Service Identity number.

18. Yes.

19. By application to Industry Canada.

20. They are not approved for installation on compulsorily fitted vessels.

21. By an audible 'alert' signal.

22. Activation requires two steps–lifting or sliding the red cover to uncover the distress button plus pressing the distress button for 5 seconds.

23. Acknowledgement on channel 70 will cancel the DSC distress message transmission.

24. Minimum of every four hours.

25. A MF-DSC radio and a 406 MHz EPIRB.

Maritime
Radio Course
Student's Notes

Appendices

NOTE: the appendices (except for appendix 3) are not examinable.

Table of Transmitting Frequencies

RBR 2 Schedule 1
(Regulation By Reference, Technical Requirements for the Operation of Mobile Stations in the Maritime Service)

Frequencies, Nature of Service, Type of Traffic and Area of Operation with Restrictions for the VHF Band in the Maritime Service

Channel	Column II Frequencies (MHz)		Column III Area of Operation								Column IV Nature of Service & Type of Traffic	Column V Restrictions (Notes and Remarks) Refer to legend for abbreviations
	Ship Transmit	Ship Receive	EC	NL	AC	GL	WC	BCC	INLD BC	INLD PRA		
1	156.050	160.650						X			PC	
2	156.100	160.700						X			PC	
3	156.150	160.750						X	X		PC	
04A	156.200	156.200	X					X			IS, SS, C, S	DFO/Canadian Coast Guard only in BCC area. Commercial fishing in EC area.
05A	156.250	156.250	X	X	X	X	X	X	X		SM	
6	156.300	156.300	X	X	X	X	X	X	X	X	IS, C, NC, S	May be used for search and rescue communications between ships and aircraft.
07A	156.350	156.350	X	X	X	X	X	X	X		IS, SS, C	
8	156.400	156.400	X			X		X			IS, C, S	Also assigned for intership in the Lake Winnipeg area.
9	156.450	156.450		X			X			X	IS, SS, C, NC, S, SM	Commercial — BCC area. May be used to communicate with aircraft and helicopters in predominantly maritime support operations.
10	156.500	156.500		X	X		X				IS, SS, C, NC, S, SM	Commercial — BCC area. May also be used for communications with aircraft engaged in coordinated search and rescue and antipollution operations.
11	156.550	156.550		X	X		X				IS, SS, C, NC, SM	VTS — BCC area. Also used for pilotage purposes.
12	156.600	156.600		X	X	X	X				IS, SS, C, NC, SM	VTS — BCC area. Port operations and pilot information and messages.
13	156.650	156.650	X	X	X	X	X	X	X		IS, C, NC, SM	VTS — BCC area. Bridge-to-bridge navigational traffic.
14	156.700	156.700			X	X		X			IS, SS,	VTS — BCC area.

Table of Transmitting Frequencies

										C, NC, SM	Port operations and pilot information and messages.
15	156.750	156.750	X	X	X	X	X	X	X		IS, SS, C, NC, SM	Port operations and Ship Movement — BCC area. All operations limited to 1-watt maximum power. May also be used for on-board communications.
16	156.800	156.800	International Distress, Safety and Calling.							AA	
17	156.850	156.850	X	X	X	X	X	X	X		IS, SS, C, NC, SM	Port operations and Ship Movement — BCC area. All operations limited to 1 watt maximum power. May also be used for on board communications.
18A	156.900	156.900	X	X	X	X	X	X	X		IS, SS, C	Towing — BCC area.
19A	156.950	156.950	X	X	X	X	X	X	X	X	IS, SS	DFO/Canadian Coast Guard. Pacific Pilots — BCC area.
20	157.000	161.600	X	X	X	X	X	X	X		SS, S, SM	Port operations only with 1 watt maximum power.
21A	157.050	157.050	X	X	X	X	X	X	X	X	IS, SS	DFO/Canadian Coast Guard only.
21B	-------	161.650	X	X	X	X	X	X	X	X	S	Continuous Marine Broadcast (CMB) service.
22A	157.100	157.100	X	X	X	X	X	X	X	X	IS, SS, C, NC	For communications between Canadian Coast Guard and non-Canadian Coast Guard stations only.
23	157.150	161.750					X	X			SS, PC	
23B	---------	161.750			X						S	Continuous Marine Broadcast (CMB) service.
24	157.200	161.800	X	X	X	X	X	X	X	X	SS, PC	
25	157.250	161.850					X				SS, PC	Also assigned for operations in the Lake Winnipeg area.
25B	-------	161.850		X							S	Continuous Marine Broadcast (CMB) service.
26	157.300	161.900	X	X	X	X	X	X	X	X	S, PC	
27	157.350	161.950		X	X		X				SS, PC	
28	157.400	162.000					X				SS, S, PC	
28B	-------	162.000		X	X						S	Continuous Marine Broadcast (CMB) service.
60	156.025	160.625					X				SS, PC	
61A	156.075	156.075	X				X				IS, SS, C	DFO/Canadian Coast Guard only in BCC area. Commercial fishing only in EC area.
62A	156.125	156.125	X				X				IS, SS	DFO/Canadian Coast Guard

Table of Transmitting Frequencies

												C	only in BCC area. Commercial fishing only in EC area.
63A	156.175	156.175							X			IS, SS, C	Tow Boats — BCC area.
64	156.225	160.825							X			SS, PC	
64A	156.225	156.225	X									IS, SS, C	Commercial fishing only.
65A	156.275	156.275	X	X	X	X	X	X	X	X		S, IS, SS, C, NC	Search and rescue and antipollution operations on the Great Lakes. Towing on the Pacific Coast. Port operations only in the St. Lawrence River areas with 1 watt maximum power. Intership in INLD PRA.
66A	156.325	156.325	X	X	X	X	X	X	X			S, IS, SS, C, NC	Port operations only in the St. Lawrence River/Great Lakes areas with 1–watt maximum power. 1 watt marina channel — BCC area.
67	156.375	156.375	X	X	X	X	X	X	X	X		S, IS, SS, C, NC	May also be used for communications with aircraft engaged in coordinated search and rescue and antipollution operations. Commercial fishing only in EC and INLD PRA areas. Pleasure craft — BCC area.
68	156.425	156.425	X	X	X	X	X	X	X	X		IS, SS, NC	For marinas, yacht clubs and pleasure craft.
69	156.475	156.475	X	X	X	X	X	X	X			IS, SS, C, NC	Commercial fishing only — EC area. Pleasure craft — BCC area.
70	156.525	156.525	Digital Selective Calling for Distress, Safety and Calling.										
71	156.575	156.575	X	X	X	X	X	X	X			S, IS, SS, SM, C, NC	Ship Movement — BCC area. Marinas and yacht clubs — EC and on Lake Winnipeg.
72	156.625	156.625	X					X				IS, C, NC	May be used to communicate with aircraft and helicopters in predominantly maritime support operations. Pleasure craft — BCC area.
73	156.675	156.675	X	X	X	X	X	X	X	X		S, IS, SS, C, NC	May also be used for communications with aircraft engaged in coordinated search and rescue and antipollution operations. Commercial fishing only in EC and INLD PRA areas.
74	156.725	156.725	X					X				IS, SS, SM, C, NC	VTS and Ship Movement — BCC area.
75	156.775	156.775	X	X	X	X	X	X	X	X		IS, SS,	Simplex port operation, ship

Table of Transmitting Frequencies

										SM, C	movement and navigation related communication only. 1 watt maximum.
76	156.825	156.825	X	X	X	X	X	X	X	X	IS, SS, SM, C	Simplex port operation, ship movement and navigation related communication only. 1 watt maximum.
77	156.875	156.875	X	X	X	X	X	X	X		S, IS, SS, SM	Pilotage — BCC area; 25 watts. Port operations only in the St. Lawrence River/Great Lakes areas with 1 watt maximum power.
78A	156.925	156.925	X				X				IS, SS, C	Fishing Industry — BCC area.
79A	156.975	156.975	X				X				IS, SS, C	Fishing Industry — BCC area.
80A	157.025	157.025	X				X				IS, SS, C	Whale Watching — BCC area.
81A	157.075	157.075	X	X	X	X	X	X	X		S, IS, SS	DFO/Canadian Coast Guard use only.
82A	157.125	157.125	X	X	X	X	X	X	X		IS, SS	DFO/Canadian Coast Guard use only.
83A	157.175	157.175	X				X				IS, SS	DFO/Canadian Coast Guard and other Government agencies.
83B	-------	161.775			X	X					S	Continuous Marine Broadcast (CMB) Service.
84	157.225	161.825					X				SS, PC	
85	157.275	161.875		X	X	X		X			SS, PC	
86	157.325	161.925					X				SS, PC	
87	157.375	157.375		X	X	X		X			IS, SM, NC	Port operation and ship movement -EC area. Pleasure craft — BCC area.
87B	161.975	161.975	X	X	X	X	X	X	X	X	**-AIS-**	Automatic Ship Identification and Surveillance System.
88	157.425	157.425		X	X	X		X			IS, SM, C	Port operation and ship movement — BCC area.
88B	162.025	162.025	X	X	X	X	X	X	X	X	**-AIS-**	Automatic Ship Identification and Surveillance System.
WX1	-------	162.550	X	X	X	X	X	X	X	X	S	Weatheradio Broadcast.
WX2	-------	162.400	X	X	X	X	X	X	X	X	S	Weatheradio Broadcast.
WX3	-------	162.475	X	X	X	X	X	X	X	X	S	Weatheradio Broadcast.

Note 1: Please refer to the Canadian Coast Guard publication *Radio Aids to Marine Navigation* (RAMN), for channels (frequencies) appropriate to your area of operation.
Note 2: For International Channel Designators please refer to Appendix 18 of the ITU *Radio Regulations*.

Table of Transmitting Frequencies

Legend (Schedule I)

Area of Operation:

- AA: All Areas
- EC (East Coast): NL, AC, GL and Eastern Arctic areas
- NL: Newfoundland and Labrador
- AC: Atlantic Coast, Gulf and St. Lawrence River up to and including Montréal
- GL: Great Lakes (including St. Lawrence above Montréal) delete accent from 'e' in Montreal
- WC (West Coast): BCC, Western Arctic and Athabasca-Mackenzie Watershed areas
- BCC: British Columbia Coast (Pacific Coast)
- INLD BC: Inland Waters of BC and the Yukon
- INLD PRA: Inland Waters of MB, SK, and AB

Nature of Service & Type of Traffic:

- IS: Intership
- SS: Ship/shore
- C: Commercial
- NC: Non-commercial
- S: Safety
- SM: Ship movement
- PC: Public correspondence
- AIS: Automatic Ship Identification and Surveillance System.
- VTS: Vessel Traffic Services

Channel Designations Explanation:

For example:

- Designated ship station **Channel 01** transmits on 156.050 MHz and receives on 160.650 MHz, and is a **duplex** channel; and
- Designated ship station **Channel 06** transmits on 156.300 MHz and receives on 156.300 MHz, and is a **Simplex** channel; and
- Designated ship station channels with the "'**A**'" extension such as **Channel 04A** are generally **simplex** channels; however,

Designated ship station **Channels 87B and 88B** are **simplex** channels and for **AIS** purposes only; while designated ship station **Channels 21B, 23B, 25B, 28B, 83B, WX1, WX2** and **WX3** are **receive only** channels for weather information.

MARINE VHF CHANNEL GROUPS - Canada, USA & International

CH	CAN	USA	INT	RECEIVE	TRANSMIT
01				160.650	156.050
01A				156.050	156.050
02				160.700	156.100
03				160.750	156.150
03A		*		156.150	156.150
04				160.800	156.200
04A				156.200	156.200
05				160.850	156.250
05A				156.250	156.250
06				156.300	156.300
07				160.950	156.350
07A				156.350	156.350
08				156.400	156.400
09		CALL		156.450	156.450
10				156.500	156.500
11				156.550	156.550
12				156.600	156.600
13	+	+		156.650	156.650
14				156.700	156.700
15	+	+	+	156.750	156.750
16				156.800	156.800
17	+	+		156.850	156.850
18				161.500	156.900
18A				156.900	156.900
19				161.550	156.950
19A				156.950	156.950
20	+			161.600	157.000
20A				157.000	157.000
21				161.650	157.050
21A		*		157.050	157.050
21B	CMB			161.650	Receive Only
22				161.700	157.100
22A				157.100	157.100
23				161.750	157.150
23A		*		157.150	157.150
24				161.800	157.200
25				161.850	157.250
25B	CMB			161.850	Receive Only
26				161.900	157.300
27				161.950	157.350
28				162.000	157.400
28B	CMB			162.000	Receive Only

+   One Watt (Low Power) Only
*   Not for use by the general public in U.S. waters.
CMB   Continuous Marine Broadcast

CH	CAN	USA	INT	RECEIVE	TRANSMIT
60				160.625	156.025
61				160.675	156.075
61A		*		156.075	156.075
62				160.725	156.125
62A				156.125	156.125
63				160.775	156.175
63A				156.175	156.175
64				160.825	156.225
64A		*		156.225	156.225
65				160.875	156.275
65A				156.275	156.275
66				160.925	156.325
66A	+			156.325	156.325
67				156.375	156.375
68				156.425	156.425
69				156.475	156.475
70	NO	VOI CE		156.525	156.525
71				156.575	156.575
72				156.625	156.625
73				156.675	156.675
74				156.725	156.725
77	+	+		156.875	156.875
78				161.525	156.925
78A				156.925	156.925
79				161.575	156.975
79A				156.975	156.975
80				161.625	157.025
80A				157.025	157.025
81				161.675	157.075
81A		*		157.075	157.075
82				161.725	157.125
82A		*		157.125	157.125
83				161.775	157.175
83A		*		157.175	157.175
83B	CMB			161.775	Receive Only
84				161.825	157.225
84A				157.225	157.225
85				161.875	157.275
85A				157.275	157.275
86				161.925	157.325
86A				157.325	157.325
87				161.975	157.375
87A				157.375	157.375
88				162.025	157.425
88A				157.425	157.425

Federal Statutes and Contraventions Act

To enforce a Federal statute, a Federal officer or inspector must first witness an infraction, then request a subpoena from a Federal judge, and then serve the subpoena. When the person or company appears before the judge, they may or may not be fined. Given the restrictions in Federal resources, it was becoming more difficult to encourage compliance with Federal statutes.

In 2000, the Federal Government created the Contraventions Act to help encourage greater compliance with all Federal statutes. This transfers the responsibility for the enforcement of the Federal statutes to the Provincial Governments. The Contraventions Act is a summary convictions act. That means for enforcement, the enforcing officer issues a ticket for the offence. The person(s) have the choice of paying the fine or challenging the issued ticket in court. With this system, the amounts for the offences are less. Most persons will acknowledge the offence, and pay the amount of the fine. This also allows for the issuing of warning tickets that can be tracked for repeat offences.

The following lists the sections of the Contraventions Act that apply to radio communications.

Note: As of 2000/03/31, the Contraventions Act applied to the following Provinces: Newfoundland, Prince Edward Island, New Brunswick, Nova Scotia, Quebec, Ontario, Manitoba, Saskatchewan, Alberta and British Columbia.

SCHEDULE IX
(Sections 1 to 3)
Radiocommunication Act

Part 1
Radiocommunication Act

Column I	Column II	Column III
Provision of Radiocommunication Act		
Item	**Short Form Description**	**Fine($)**
1. 4(1) and 10(1)*(a)*	*(c)* Operate a radio apparatus without a radio authorization	Corporation 500 Individual 250
	(d) Operate a radio apparatus in contravention of the conditions of the authorization	Corporation 500 Individual 250
4. 5(1)*(1)* and 10(1)*(c)*	*(a)* Contravene an order of the Minister to cease operation of the radio apparatus until such time as it can be operated without causing harmful interference	Corporation 500 Individual 250
	(b) Contravene an order of the Minister to cease operation of the radio apparatus until such time as it can be affected by harmful interference	Corporation 500 Individual 250

PART II

Radiocommunication Regulations

Column I	Column II	Column III
Provision of Radiocommunication Regulations		
Item	**Short Form Description**	**Fine($)**
1. 18	Fail to identify broadcasting station as prescribed	250
8. 30	Operate authorized radio apparatus contrary to the terms and conditions of the authorization	Corporation 500 Individual 250
10. 32(1)	Transmit superfluous signals	250
11. 33	Operate a radio apparatus without a radio operator certificate as prescribed	100
12. 34	Permit a person to operate a radio apparatus without the person having a radio operator certificate as prescribed	100
14. 39*(b)*	Install radio apparatus on behalf of another person contrary to the terms and conditions of the licence	Corporation 500 Individual 250
15. 41	Failure by person who has a radio licence to identify the radio station as prescribed	Corporation 500 Individual 250
23. 53*(2)*	Operate radio apparatus contrary to the Minister's order	Corporation 500 Individual 250

Time Zone Comparison

UTC	Co-ordinated Universal Time
NST	Newfoundland Standard Time
AST	Atlantic Standard Time
EST	Eastern Standard Time
CST	Central Standard Time
MST	Mountain Standard Time
PST	Pacific Standard Time

Previous Day ▨
Current Day ☐

To convert from Co-ordinated Universal Time (UTC) to local standard time, look opposite UTC under the appropriate column below. When going East to West, subtract the difference. For corresponding Daylight Saving Time, add one hour to time shown.

UTC	NST	AST	EST	CST	MST	PST
(-0)	(-3.5)	(-4)	(-5)	(-6)	(-7)	(-8)
0100	2130	2100	2000	1900	1800	1700
0200	2230	2200	2100	2000	1900	1800
0300	2330	2300	2200	2100	2000	1900
0400	0030	0000	2300	2200	2100	2000
0500	0130	0100	0000	2300	2200	2100
0600	0230	0200	0100	0000	2300	2200
0700	0330	0300	0200	0100	0000	2300
0800	0430	0400	0300	0200	0100	0000
0900	0530	0500	0400	0300	0200	0100
1000	0630	0600	0500	0400	0300	0200
1100	0730	0700	0600	0500	0400	0300
1200	0830	0800	0700	0600	0500	0400
1300	0930	0900	0800	0700	0600	0500
1400	1030	1000	0900	0800	0700	0600
1500	1130	1100	1000	0900	0800	0700
1600	1230	1200	1100	1000	0900	0800
1700	1330	1300	1200	1100	1000	0900
1800	1430	1400	1300	1200	1100	1000
1900	1530	1500	1400	1300	1200	1100
2000	1630	1600	1500	1400	1300	1200
2100	1730	1700	1600	1500	1400	1300
2200	1830	1800	1700	1600	1500	1400
2300	1930	1900	1800	1700	1600	1500
0000	2030	2000	1900	1800	1700	1600

Radio Station Licence Sample (if required)

 Industry Industrie
Canada Canada

RADIO LICENCE

Issued under the authority of the Minister, Industry Canada in accordance with the Radiocommunications Act
and Regulations made thereunder

ISSUE DATE	EXPIRY DATE	ACCOUNT NO.
April 1, 1998	March 31, 1999	

RADIOCOMMUNICATION USER

B24758   ICLICE   2128

J

THIS LICENCE AUTHORIZES THE OPERATION OF THE STATIONS LISTED BELOW

NUMBER TYPE	CALLSIGN	NAME OF VESSEL	SERVICES APPENDICES
		LICENSEES LICENSED VESSEL	M
MOBILE			

LICENCE CONDITIONS

THE RADIO STATION DESCRIBED ON THIS LICENCE IS AUTHORIZED TO OPERATE ON FREQUENCIES LISTED IN
RADIOCOMMUNICATION INFORMATION CIRCULAR, RIC13 PUBLISHED BY INDUSTRY CANADA, AND
ON FREQUENCIES LISTED IN THE RADIO AIDS TO MARINE NAVIGATION, PACIFIC, ATLANTIC, AND GREAT LAKES
PUBLISHED BY THE DEPARTMENT OF TRANSPORT, COAST GUARD. THE USE OF THESE FREQUENCIES IS SUBJECT TO
LIMITATIONS OF AREA, NATURE OF SERVICE, AND TYPE OF TRAFFIC DESCRIBED IN THESE PUBLICATIONS.

POWER IN KW

VHF 0.025

SERVICES

M   MARITIME

INQUIRIES CONCERNING THIS RADIO LICENCE SHOULD BE DIRECTED TO INDUSTRY CANADA DISTRICT OFFICE,
451 TALBOT STREET, ROOM 1112, LONDON, ONTARIO, N6A 5C9, TEL. (519) 645-4336 OR TOLL FREE 1-800-265-1273.
(DISPONIBLE EN FRANÇAIS)   (SEE REVERSE SIDE)
2128   ICLIC   IE   Page 1 of 1

XIII

EXEMPTION OF RADIO APPARATUS ON BOARD A SHIP OR VESSEL

15.2 (1) This section applies in respect of a ship or vessel that is:

(a) registered or licensed under an Act of Parliament; or

(b) owned by, or under the direction or control of, Her Majesty in right of Canada or a province.

(2) A radio apparatus that is operated on board a ship or vessel in the performance of the maritime service or the radiodetermination service is exempt from subsection 4(1) of the Act, in respect of a radio licence, if:

(a) the operation of the radio apparatus occurs when:

(i) the ship or vessel is within Canada,

(ii) the ship or vessel is outside Canada and the territory of another country, or

(iii) the ship or vessel is in the territory of another country with which Canada has entered into a reciprocal agreement that confers similar privileges on Canadians;

(b) the operation or the radio apparatus is in accordance with the technical requirements for moble stations operating in the maritime service specified in Section 34.2; and

(c) the radio apparatus meets the applicable standards. SOR/99-107

Safety information

Sail Plan

If you are planning a cruise or trip on coastal or inland waters, leave a *Sail Plan* with family, a neighbour or a friend.

A Sail Plan is a trip outline and provides information which will assist the Canadian Coast Guard in the event you become overdue, and/or need to be located.

A Sail Plan should include:

(a) Complete *description* of your vessel, (type, length, colour, special markings, etc.)
(b) The *number* of persons aboard,
(c) Your planned *routing* or *itinerary*,
(d) If *radio-equipped*, the *type* (VHF, MF, etc) and *channels* monitored,
(e) The *telephone number* of the appropriate Rescue Coordination Centre or the Coast Guard Radio Station nearest to your community.

If you become overdue, or an emergency situation occurs at home, the responsible person holding your Sail Plan may contact Coast Guard through the number you have shown.

Canadian Coast Guard Radio will commence a communications search on radio. At the same time, the Rescue Coordination Centre will be advised in the event a more intensive search is required.

If at any time you should divert from your filed Sail Plan, the change should be *reported* to the persons responsible for holding the original Sail Plan, so that they may amend it accordingly.

Figure A-1: CCG and CCGA Logos

Safety Inspections

Pleasure craft boaters should be aware of the importance of keeping their vessel's safety equipment up to date and in good working order.

The Canadian Power & Sail Squadrons offers free courtesy safety inspections for all pleasure craft vessels in Canada. In the event that your vessel does not pass the inspection, the CPS personnel will advise you what is the proper safety equipment required for your particular vessel. Once you have obtained the needed equipment, that portion of the inspection may be reviewed so that you can obtain a pass.

If your vessel does pass, a sticker will be provided indicating that you have passed the inspection.

This is a courtesy inspection. It is not a police action. Its purpose is to help you to be safe and to assist you to be aware of what is needed.

This is done entirely on a volunteer basis.

To obtain the service, contact your nearest CPS squadron or to receive contact information with someone in your nearest squadron, please call CPS at
1-888-CPS-BOAT (1-888-277-2628) or in the Toronto area call
(416)-293-2438.

Obtaining a MMSI Number

To apply for a MMSI number for your vessel, you can go onto the Internet and use your Internet browser to go to the following site.

http://www.ic.gc.ca/eic/site/sd-sd.nsf/eng/00009.html or Google for "MMSI Canada".

You will be asked to choose an 'Annex', which is the terminology used to describe a form to be filled out. Each Annex comes two ways, as PDF file or as a WPD file.

If your vessel is one that does not require a radio station licence (a pleasure craft, voluntarily fitted) and you will only have a VHF/DSC radio on board, then choose Annex A.

If your vessel is one that is required to have a radio station licence (commercial vessels, compulsorily fitted) or if it has additional radio equipment (more than just a VHF/DSC radio), select Annex B.

If you are applying for a group (fleet) MMSI, then one person applies on behalf of the group. Use Annex D for a group MMSI number.

If you are a coast station (e.g. a yacht club, a marina, a shore-based business), use Annex C.

You also need to decide if you want the form that has to be filled out to be in Word Perfect format or as a PFD. If you want to use a PDF, you need a PDF reader (or a PDF writer such as Acrobat). You may also use the PDF version if your word processor works with PFD files. If you do not already have such a reader, there are numerous PDF readers available for free download or for purchase on the Internet:

- Adobe Reader
- Foxit Reader
- Xpdf
- eXPert PDF Reader

If you prefer to use the Word Perfect version you may use it with Word Perfect or a program that recognizes Word Perfect documents.

You will be asked to fill in some abbreviations (Vessel Codes) which are to be found on Annex E. It is suggested that you download Annex E first so that you can easily find the codes.

When filling out the form you will be asked for the vessel's General Classification (this field is mandatory). On Annex E you will find the General Classifications to be:

Fishing vessel – FV,
Naval ship – NS,
Pleasure craft – PL,
River vessel – NF,
Merchant ship – MM,
Official service ship – GV,
Rescue vessel – SV,
Unspecified – XX

Most of us will choose PL (pleasure craft).

You will also be asked to enter the code(s) for individual classifications. You may get the codes from Annex E. Most users will select MTB (Motor Boat) or VLR (Sailing Ship). Some users may include SLO (Sloop) or YAT (Yacht) Do review the other options on Annex E to see if they apply. You may enter more than one code if applicable.

If the vessel's length is 12 metres (39 feet) or less, fill in the Gross Tonnage as follows…

Length Overall	Gross Tonnage
less than 8.5 m	5
8.5 m or more but less than 9 m	6
9 m or more but less than 9.5 m	7
9.5 m or more but less than 10 m	8
10 m or more but less than 10.5 m	10
10.5 m or more but less than 11 m	11
11 m or more but less than 11.5 m	13
11.5 m or more but not exceeding 12 m	15

Over 12 metres, enter the actual gross tonnage.

Fields on the form which have a checkmark are mandatory, you must fill them in. Fields which are marked with an X need to be filled in only if an MMSI number has already been issued (e.g., you are modifying the information, making a change of name, etc.).

Once you have downloaded the proper form (Annex), print it and fill it out. Then take it in person, mail or fax it to the nearest Industry Canada office.

To determine which Industry Canada office is nearest to you, please consult Radiocommunication Information Circular 66, Addresses and Telephone Numbers of Regional and District Offices as shown in the following pages.

Regional and District offices of Industry Canada—Spectrum Management

Western Region

Manitoba District Office
4th Floor
400 St. Mary Avenue
Winnipeg MB R3C 4K5
Telephone: 1-800-665-3421
Fax: 204-984-6045
Email: spectrum.winnipeg.district@ic.gc.ca
(By appointment only)

Central and Northern Alberta District Office
Room 725, Canada Place
9700 Jasper Avenue
Edmonton AB T5J 4C3
Telephone: 1-800-461-2646
Fax: 780-495-6501
Email: spectrum.edmonton@ic.gc.ca
(By appointment only)

Southern Alberta District Office
Room 400
639 Fifth Avenue S.W.
Calgary AB T2P 0M9
Telephone: 1-800-267-9401
Fax: 403-292-4295
Email: spectrum.calgary@ic.gc.ca
(By appointment only)

Saskatchewan District

Regina Office
Room 600
1945 Hamilton Street
Regina SK S4P 2C7
Telephone: 1-877-510-7875
Fax: 306-780-6506
Email: spectrum.regina@ic.gc.ca
(By appointment only)

Saskatoon Office
7th Floor
123 2nd Avenue South
Saskatoon SK S7K 7E6
Telephone: 1-877-783-7757
Fax: 306-975-4231
Email: spectrum.saskatoon@ic.gc.ca
(By appointment only)

Northwest Territories and Nunavut

(Administered by Saskatoon Office)
7th Floor
123 2nd Avenue South
Saskatoon SK S7K 7E6
Telephone: 1-877-783-7757
Fax: 306-975-4231
Email: spectrum.saskatoon@ic.gc.ca
(By appointment only)

Interior British Columbia and Yukon District:

Okanagan-Kootenay Office
Room 603
1726 Dolphin Avenue
Kelowna BC V1Y 9R9
Telephone: 250-470-5026 or 1-800-667-3780
Fax: 250-470-5045
Email: kelowna.district@ic.gc.ca
(By appointment only)

Northern British Columbia and Yukon Office
Room 203
280 Victoria Street
Prince George BC V2L 4X3
Telephone: 250-561-5291 or 1-800-667-3780
Fax: 250-561-5290
Email: princegeorge.district@ic.gc.ca
(By appointment only)

Yukon Field Office
Room 205
300 Main Street
Whitehorse YT Y1A 2B5
Telephone: 867-667-5102
Fax: 867-393-6711
Email: jeff.stanhope@ic.gc.ca
(By appointment only)

Coastal British Columbia District:

Lower Mainland Office
Suite 1700
13401 - 108 Avenue
Surrey BC V3T 5V6
Tel: 604-586-2521
Fax: 604-586-2528
Email: vancouver.district@ic.gc.ca
(By appointment only)

Vancouver Island Office
Room430
1230 Government Street
Victoria BC V8W 3M4
Tel: 250-363-3803
Fax: 250-363-0208
Email: victoria.district@ic.gc.ca
(By appointment only)

Quebec Region

Quebec Regional Office
Sun Life Building
1155 Metcalfe Street, Room 950
Montréal, Quebec H3B 2V6
Telephone: 1-855-784-8282
Fax: 514-283-5157
Email: spectre.region.quebec@ic.gc.ca
(By appointment only)

Western Quebec District Office

Montréal Service Centre
Sun Life Building
1155 Metcalfe Street, Room 950
Montréal, Quebec H3B 2V6
Telephone: 1-855-784-8282
Fax: 514-283-5157
Email: spectre.region.quebec@ic.gc.ca
(By appointment only)

Gatineau Service Centre
Room 222
975 Saint-Joseph Boulevard
Gatineau QC J8Z 1W8
Telephone: 1-855-784-8282
Fax: 514-283-5157
Email: spectre.region.quebec@ic.gc.ca
(By appointment only)

Val-d'Or Service Centre
380 Lamaque Boulevard
P.O. Box 695
Val-d'Or QC J9P 4P6
Telephone: 1-855-784-8282
Fax: 514-283-5157
Email: spectre.region.quebec@ic.gc.ca
(By appointment only)

Eastern Quebec District Office

Quebec Service Centre
702-1550 d'Estimauville Avenue
Québec QC G1J 0C4
Telephone: 1-855-784-8282
Fax: 514-283-5157
Email: spectre.region.quebec@ic.gc.ca
(By appointment only)

Sherbrooke Service Centre
Room 600
2665 King Street West
Sherbrooke QC J1L 2G5
Telephone: 1-855-784-8282

Fax: 514-283-5157
Email: spectre.region.quebec@ic.gc.ca
(By appointment only)

Atlantic and Ontario Region

New Brunswick/Prince Edward Island District Office

3rd Floor
Customs Building
189 Prince William Street
Saint John NB E2L 2B9
Telephone: 1-855-465-6307
Fax: 506-636-4339
Email: SaintJohn.District@ic.gc.ca
(By appointment only)

Nova Scotia District Office

50 Brown Avenue
Dartmouth NS B3B 1X8
Telephone: 1-855-465-6307
Fax: 902-426-1000
Email: Dartmouth.district@ic.gc.ca
(By appointment only)

Newfoundland and Labrador District Office

P.O. Box 8950
10th Floor
John Cabot Building
10 Barter's Hill
St. John's NL A1B 3R9
Telephone: 1-855-465-6307
Fax: 709-772-4890
Email: St.John s.District@ic.gc.ca
(By appointment only)

Toronto District Office

Room 909
55 St. Clair Avenue East
Toronto ON M4T 1M2
Telephone: 1-855-465-6307
Fax: 416-954-3553
Email: spectrum.toronto@ic.gc.ca

Hours of operations: 8:30 a.m. - 4:30 p.m.
(By appointment only)

Central and Western Ontario District Office

Suite 100
4475 North Service Road
Burlington, Ontario
L7L 4X7
Telephone: 1-855-465-6307
Fax: 905-639-6551
Email: spectrum.cwod@ic.gc.ca
Hours of Operation: 8:30 a.m. - 4:30 p.m.
(By appointment only)

Eastern and Northern Ontario District

2 Queen Street East
Sault Ste. Marie ON P6A 1Y3
Telephone: 1-855-465-6307
Fax: 705-941-4607
Email: spectrum.sault-ste-marie@ic.gc.ca
Hours of Operation: 8:30 a.m. - 4:30 p.m.
(By appointment only)

Security requirements when visiting United States waters

In the wake of the events of September 11, 2001, United States authorities have established a number of new homeland security requirements. Anyone operating a boat in U.S. waters must abide by these requirements.

U.S. naval vessel protection zone

Other vessels are prohibited from passing within 100 yards (92 metres) of any U.S. naval vessel. If it is essential for another vessel to enter this zone in order to ensure a safe passage, that vessel must first contact the U.S. naval vessel in question (or its U.S. Coast Guard escort vessel or the official patrol, if applicable), using VHF/FM radio Channel 16; and it may proceed only as directed.

Outside this 100-yard zone, other vessels approaching a U.S. naval vessel within 500 yards (458 metres) are required to operate at the minimum speed necessary to maintain a safe course, and to proceed as directed by the commanding officer of the U.S. naval vessel in question or the official patrol.

If any vessel fails to abide by these requirements, it is subject to immediate boarding by U.S. authorities and the violators face a prison term of up to six years and a fine of up to $250,000 U.S. dollars.

As well, approaching certain other commercial vessels may result in immediate boarding by U.S. authorities.

Other U.S. security zones

There are several other kinds of security zones of which boaters visiting the U.S. must be aware. Listed below are specific security warnings transcribed from U.S. Coast Guard publications:

- "Observe and avoid all security zones. Avoid commercial port operation areas, especially those that involve military, cruise-line, or petroleum facilities. Observe and avoid other restricted areas near dams, power plants, etc. Violators will be perceived as a threat, and will face a quick, determined, and severe response."

- "Do not stop or anchor beneath bridges or in the channel. If you do, then expect to be boarded by law enforcement officials."

- "Keep a sharp eye out for anything that looks peculiar or out of the ordinary. Report all activities that seem suspicious to the local authorities, the Coast Guard, or the port or marina security. Do not approach or challenge those acting in a suspicious manner."

Using current information

Anyone intending to operate a boat in U.S. waters should—before leaving Canada—obtain the latest update of the U.S. homeland security requirements set out above, as well as full information regarding such other matters as U.S. immigration and customs requirements, U.S. boat licensing requirements, and U.S. maritime VHF radio licensing requirements.

Both the U.S. Coast Guard and U.S. Immigration and Customs Enforcement are part of the U.S. Departmentof Homeland Security. Its website is <http://www.dhs.gov/>.

Radio Aids to Marine Navigation

The Radio Aids to Marine Navigation (RAMN) is a publication of the Canadian Coast Guard. It is available in two volumes. One volume covers from Manitoba to the Atlantic coast; the other covers Western Canada.

It is published each April and may be updated in the monthly edition of Notices to Mariners.

RAMN contains a great deal of information which involves mariners, including proposed changes to navigation, lists of all Coast Guard stations, the frequencies they use and more.

This publication is available in printed form from authorized (CHS) charts dealers.

It is also available to download for free from the Internet at www.ccg-gcc.gc.ca/eng/CCG/MCTS_Radio_Aids

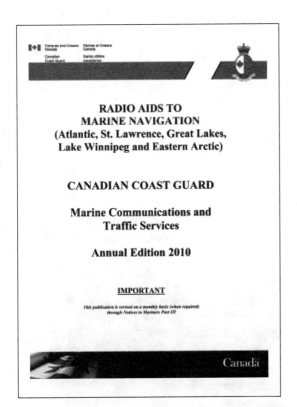

Automatic Identification System (AIS)

Introduction

The Automatic Identification System (AIS) (also known as Universal Automatic Identification System (UAIS) or Ship Automatic Identification System (SAIS)) is used by vessels primarily to locate and identify nearby vessels for collision avoidance. Shore-based Vessel Traffic Systems (VTS) may also use AIS information to monitor vessel positions.

AIS uses VHF radio signals to transmit navigational and other data between vessels, and between vessels and shore stations. This digital data is transmitted alternately on Marine VHF channels 87B (161.975 MHz) and 88B (162.025 MHz). As AIS uses channels in the Marine VHF band, the signal range will be similar to that of VHF voice communications. An AIS receiver will often detect targets that are hidden from radar by intervening land. The AIS system allows shore-based repeater stations to be used to expand coverage beyond line of sight.

AIS uses a system called Self-Organizing Time Division Multiple Access (SOTDMA) to minimize interference between transmitters. In this system, each minute is divided into 2250 time slots, and any transmission will only occupy one slot. In each transmission, a transponder will announce the slot that it will use for its next transmission. The transponder keeps track of what slots have recently been announced so that it can select a free slot for its own transmissions.

An AIS receiver will receive and decode data from all vessels within range. The data may be displayed on a text display, but most often will be shown as icons on an electronic charting system or radar screen.

A full AIS transponder includes both receiver and transmitter, but receive-only units are also available. If you have a receive-only unit, you will be aware of other vessels, but your vessel will not appear on their AIS displays.

Carriage Requirements

SOLAS vessels (vessels required to comply with the International Convention for the Safety of Life at Sea) over 300 gross tons, and passenger vessels, engaged in international voyages have been required to carry Class A AIS transponders since 2004. Since July 1 2008 Canada requires that ships, other than fishing vessels, of 500 tons or more that are not engaged in an international voyage be fitted with AIS equipment.

All commercial vessels using the St. Lawrence Seaway have been required to carry AIS since March 2003. On the Seaway, the information provided by AIS allows better scheduling of lockages and other activities than was possible previously. Shore stations use the AIS system to transmit weather and other information to participating vessels.

Transponders

There are two classes of AIS transponder available. A Class A transponder meets the requirements for carriage on compulsorily-equipped vessels, while the simpler Class B transponder is intended for use on voluntarily-equipped vessels such as pleasure craft.

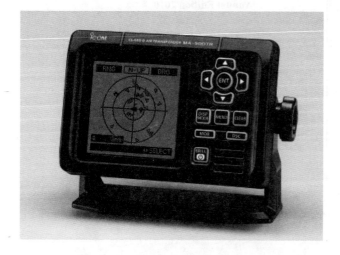

Figure 10.1: An AIS Transponder

A Class A transponder includes a GPS receiver, a tuneable transmitter, and two tuneable AIS receivers. It also has a Channel 70 DSC receiver. When AIS was first implemented, some countries had other services assigned to Channels 87B and 88B, so they required a means to shift the AIS transmitter and receivers to alternate channels. This was done by having a shore station broadcast commands on Channel 70. A Class A transponder also has a text display and keyboard to permit the user to enter voyage data, set the navigation status, and to send text messages to other vessels. Class A transponders cost U.S. $3,000 or more.

The display can show data from other vessels in a text format, or on a blank plotter screen.

Class B

A Class B transponder is somewhat simpler than a Class A unit, and its transmitter is only 2 watts, rather than the 12.5 watts of a Class A transponder. As a Class B transponder does not transmit navigation status or voyage details, a keyboard and display is not required for normal operation. It is assumed that the transponder data output will be fed to a chart display system or radar which will display the AIS targets and other data. Class B transponders are available from U.S. $800. These units come with a PC-based program for configuration, and to display received data.

AIS Receivers

Figure 10.2: AIS receiver

AIS receivers, without the transmitter found in transponders, are also available. A single channel receiver without a display can be purchased for $200, while dual channel receivers are about $400. One

manufacturer makes a receiver called an 'AIS RADAR' which includes a graphic LCD display to show the relative positions of AIS targets. Despite the name, this unit is only an AIS receiver/display with no radar function.

Message Types

An AIS transponder transmits two primary types of message. The Position Report contains frequently changing data such as position and speed, and the Static and Voyage Data message contains vessel details and some details of the current voyage.

Navigational Status is selected from several pre-defined items: underway using engine, at anchor, not under command, restricted manoeuvrability, etc.

Type of ship and cargo is selected from several pre-defined types: cargo, passenger, tug, etc. This field also includes a flag to indicate the vessel is carrying dangerous cargo.

The reported position of a vessel is actually the position of its GPS antenna.

Figures 10.3 and 10.4 show vessels in Vancouver Harbour, which can be seen at the upper right of the CPS Training Chart.

In addition to the messages described above, there are message formats defined for Search and Rescue aircraft position reports, Aids-to-Navigation reports, weather and safety messages from coast stations and other items.

AIS Display

As mentioned above, the AIS data is most often displayed as icons representing the vessels shown on an electronic chart or radar display. A common display shows a small triangle indicating the vessel's heading with lines indicating speed and direction of turn (see figure 10.3). Moving a cursor over the icon will display useful navigation data, see figure 10.4, and clicking on the icon will display full data on the vessel (see figure

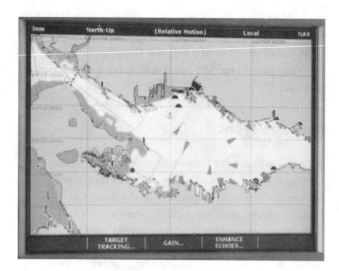

Figure 10.3 AIS Display showing vectors for two vessels

Figure 10.4: AIS Display of Navigation Data

10.5). When zoomed in to a large scale, the size of the icon may vary depending on the size of the vessel.

Most display systems will continuously calculate the time and distance of the closest approach (TCPA and CPA) for each AIS target. In addition, it will change the colour of the icon and provide an alarm if a target is likely to come within a selectable alarm distance. In a busy harbour where there are many AIS users, these warnings may become annoying, and can usually be turned off.

Figures 10-3, 4 and 5 are of a Raymarine C80 multifunction display. On this system, AIS targets are shown as triangles pointing in the direction of the vessel's heading. The system still monitors targets that are not moving and will warn if they pose a danger. Those targets will show the triangle icon. A selected or 'active' icon will show vectors indicating heading, speed and rate of turn.

In Figure 10-4, the cursor has been placed over one target, and the heading, speed, distance at the Closest Point of Approach (CPA) and the Time of Closest Point of Approach (TCPA) are shown.

In Figure 10.5, you have pressed the View Full AIS Data key, and find that the target is the 'Burrard Beaver' (one of three passenger ferries known as 'The Seabus' that travel across the harbour between downtown Vancouver and North Vancouver). You can see most of the data listed above for the Position and Static Data messages. Because the vessel makes many short trips across the harbour each day, the crew hasn't entered the destination, ETA or navigation status.

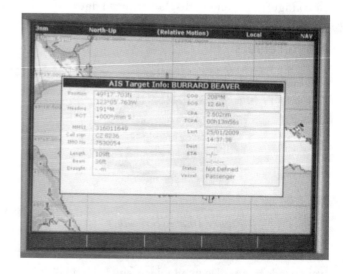

Figure 10.5: Full data display

Figure 10.6: Tiki Navigator Display

Figure 10.7: Tiki Navigator Full Data Display

The chart display program 'Tiki Navigator' shows AIS targets as circles (see figure 10.6). Depending on the display scale, larger vessels may be shown as a rectangle which indicates the actual size of the vessel. Vessels that are underway have lines representing their speed and direction.

In Tiki Navigator, placing the cursor (the black hand) over a target will bring up the yellow box at the right of the screen with limited data on the target.

If you click on the grey box, the full vessel information is produced as well as a list of other AIS targets that have been received (see figure 10.7). The distance and bearing shown in this box are measured from the author's vessel, moored on the south shore of English Bay (top right corner of the CPS Training Chart). As the Costal Reliance is moving away from the author's vessel, there is no CPA or TCPA given.

The CD that accompanies this course.

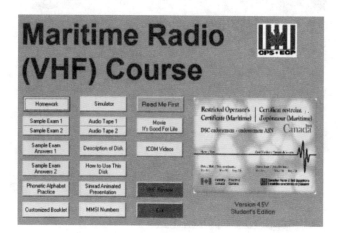

A CD comes with this course and can be used in a PC. Portions of the CD will run on a MAC if the computer has PowerPoint, etc. Some portions of the CD will only run on a MAC that has a PC emulator or an operating system that runs PC programs.

The CD has a number of features to help you learn the material in this course. One of the most useful is the DSC simulator.

The following will give you a preview of what is on the CD.

Homework

Double click the selection 'Homework' and you will access a program that is very useful for home study.

The program shows a menu which lists the sections of the book.

Select the section you wish to work on and a question appears which has multiple-choice answers. Click with the mouse on the answer you wish to choose. You will be told if you selected the correct answer. If a wrong answer is chosen, it will be corrected with a short explanation.

When you have finished all the questions for the section, you will see your score of right and wrong answers, what percentage you had right and you are given the chance to redo the incorrectly answered questions.

We suggest you read the section in the manual one day and use this homework program the next day. Then, redo any wrong questions over again until they are all correct. Each time the program is run, the answers are randomly sorted so that they are not always in the same order.

The program may be run as often as you wish. This homework exercise is a great learning tool.

Sample examination

Included is a practice exam similar to the real one. It has 25 questions. Part One of the real exam has 60 questions; a pass is 42 correct answers. Part Two of the real exam consists of three oral questions administered by the examiner in order to verify your knowledge of the phonetic alphabet and your ability to send priority calls. As with the real exam, it is multiple choice, four possible answers per question.

A number of different exams will be given to students on examination day, in order that no two students sitting beside each other will have the same exam.

Sample examination answers

You may read the answers in this section of the CD. The correct answer is underlined and a reference to the section number in the manual is shown. We suggest that if you get an answer wrong, you look up the appropriate section in the manual.

Audio Files (MP3 type)

An audio teaching file has been reproduced here to demonstrate some of the uses of maritime radio and the proper form of different types of calls.

This can be used as is, and it can be copied onto a MP3 player. It is useful if your car radio can play a CD. It contains a wealth of information about maritime radio in general and also contains a number of examples indicating the correct way to make various types of calls. It also demonstrates some common errors in making calls and explains why they should not be used.

There are some problems with this file. It was produced over twenty years ago and some changes have been made in the regulations since then. For example, not all radio stations require licensing now, but they did at the time this tape was produced. Back then, a government manual was available which has been replaced by the CPS Maritime Radio Course. The proper phonetic for the number nine is now pronounced 'nine', not 'niner'. Operators are now 'certified', not 'licensed'. We hope to re-create this tape soon, but for now, please be aware that the tape has these discrepancies from current practice.

You may listen to the recording right on a computer. All Microsoft systems since 1995 have a program called Microsoft Media Player. Just by clicking on this CD's Audio Tape button, the program will be activated. If a computer is missing an up-to-date version of this program, it is available free of charge from Microsoft's website on the Internet.

Phonetic Alphabet Trainer

The program displays a letter of the alphabet, then after a pause, it gives you a chance to say the phonetic word. It then displays the phonetic word. Repeated use of this program will give the practice needed to learn the phonetic alphabet. We suggest you start with this program to become familiar with the internationally approved version of the alphabet. Then, while driving your car, practice, by saying out loud phonetically, car licence plate numbers and street signs.

The program begins by going through the alphabet in regular order, after which it mixes up the letters.

Movie, it's Good For Life!

There is a fifteen-minute movie available on the disk. As stated above, the movie can be played on all computers using Microsoft's Windows 95 or later.

Review

This question and answer type program gives you the opportunity to see how ready you are for the exam. It asks a question (sometimes in a fill-in-the-blank format) then shows the answer. This also acts a pre-exam review.

DSC Simulator

Learn to use the various controls and capabilities of a DSC radio.

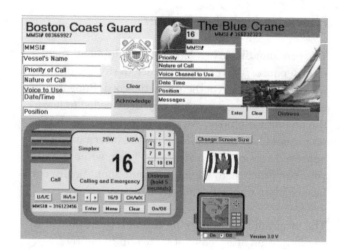

A real radio has an owner's manual and so does this simulator. Read the manual and become acquainted with its features. Take the Cruise of the Simul from New Brunswick down the Massachusetts coast.

Animated Presentation

We have an excellent animated presentation on the CD courtesy of Simrad. It explains the principles of GMDSS.

ICOM Videos

We have some videos courtesy of ICOM UNIVERSITY.

These presentations provide further explanations of some concepts of Digital Selective Calling.

Customized Booklet

It is one thing to learn the rules and procedures. It may be another to properly present them on the air when a situation occurs. This program helps you to create a customized, tabbed, water-resistant booklet on your home computer. You input personal details such as the name of your boat. When needed, you use the tabs to quickly locate the proper format for calls such as Distress, Mayday Relay, etc. The calls are customized for your vessel.

This booklet is an invaluable aid if a passenger has to use your radio.

MMSI Numbers

This section contains help about how to obtain an MMSI number.

In conclusion

We hope the material on this CD will help you to obtain your Radio Operator's Certificate (Maritime).

Students who take this course will also likely be interested in taking modules in the Electronic Navigation courses, such as GPS and Electronic Charting, Depth Sounder and Radar.

MF/HF and Single Sideband

There are various methods designers of radios use to put voice onto radio waves. The process of doing so is called 'modulation'. The more common form of modulation used on radio broadcast bands is called AM, (Amplitude Modulation). This was the form of modulation used ever since the early 1900's and it is still in common use today on the AM commercial broadcast band. About 50 years ago a better method called FM, (Frequency Modulation) was put to use. It is used on the FM commercial band. This became popular because it was not affected as much by lightning interference (which causes static) and provided clearer music. We use FM modulation on the VHF maritime radio band.

Another form of modulation is called SSB, (Single SideBand, suppressed carrier). This is a very effective form of modulation. Without getting technical, it makes a radio signal appear much stronger. In fact, it behaves as if the signal were eight times stronger than if the signal were being broadcast using AM.

Figure 12-1: A SSB (MF/HF) Transceiver

Today we use SSB on most of the MF/HF maritime radio frequencies.

The medium frequency band (MF) covers 2 MHz – 2.85 MHz, while the high frequency (HF) range covers eight bands between 4 MHz and 26 MHz (often called 'short wave'). In the 2 MHz band, radio waves tend to follow the earth's curvature (called ground wave propagation), giving usable ranges of 60 miles during the day, and increasing to 200 miles at night. At higher frequencies, the ground wave becomes less effective, and we rely on sky waves, which are reflected by ionized layers in the upper atmosphere. For any frequency, there is generally a 'skip zone' (where no signals can be heard) between the limit of usable ground wave coverage and the location where the first reflected signals can be received. The height and density of the ionized layers vary through the day, allowing higher frequencies to be reflected during the day, and lower frequencies at night. By selecting the appropriate times and frequencies, world-wide communication is possible. A full discussion of HF propagation is beyond the scope of this course. More information can be found in amateur radio publications.

The MF and HF bands can be used for voice communications between vessels or between vessels and shore stations, some of which can provide connections to the telephone system. There are also radio, telex and email services available on these bands.

Since most marine MF/HF transceivers can also cover the MF/HF Amateur bands, many ocean cruisers obtain Amateur Radio licences, and use the amateur bands to keep in touch with other cruisers, and to make 'phone patches'. There are also email services on the amateur bands.

At one time it was likely that you would buy a MF radio and also a HF radio. Today, both bands are covered in a single package, that is, the same radio is capable of transmitting and receiving MF and HF frequencies.

Channel 16 is the international calling and distress frequency for VHF. 2182 kHz has a similar purpose for MF. Just as we can use Channel 16 for 'listening out' on VHF, we can use 2182 kHz for listening out on the MF band. The introduction of DSC removed the dependence on Channel 16 for VHF and those with DSC may now use Channel 70 for the same purpose. Similarly, those with DSC on their MF radios now use 2187.5 kHz rather than 2182 kHz.

Note, VHF uses channel numbers. When you select a channel, the radio automatically sets the frequency

for transmitting. This frequency may differ from one country to another, hence the need for a mode switch. The radio also selects a frequency for receiving. If the transmitting and receiving channels are the same, that is called Simplex. If they differ, it is called Duplex (see RBR 2 in Appendix 1). In general, MF and HF radios do not use channel numbers, they use the frequency number such as 2182 kHz.

For more information on MF/HF, see Module 1, section 1.1.10 of this manual and also section 1.1.4 for information on 'radio silence periods'.

Propagation and Antennas

Most of us will use VHF radios, which operate in the 156 – 162 MHz band. At these frequencies the useable range of communications is usually described as 'line of sight', although signals are reflected by land masses and do bend around obstacles to some extent, giving a somewhat better range than pure line-of-sight would imply. Typical ranges between vessels are 15 to 20 miles. Shore station antennas are usually on tall towers or mountain tops, giving them a considerably greater range.

The maximum permitted power of a transmitter on a vessel is 25 watts, and is considered sufficient to reach any vessel within the line-of-sight range. All marine radios are required to have a means to reduce the transmitter power to 1 watt, which is to be used for communication with nearby stations. Always use the minimum power necessary for communications with nearby stations as that will permit distant stations to use the same channel without interference.

VHF antennas are available having gains (efficiency) of 3, 6, or 9 dB relative to a theoretical antenna that would radiate equally well in all directions. A dB or decibel is a measure of relative power or signal strength. A gain of 3 dB is a doubling of power. A real antenna will direct most transmitted signal at right angles to the antenna element, and little or no signal off the ends of the element.

A 3 dB antenna has a very broad pattern – it will still transmit a reasonable signal up to 80 degrees above or below horizontal, if the antenna is vertical. 3 dB antennas are normally used on sailboats, mounted at the top of the mast. Their wide pattern provides a good signal towards the horizon even when the boat is heeled. They are small, only about 1 m (3 ft) long, and light weight (always desirable on a sailboat). The high mounting point should compensate for the lower gain, and loss of signal in the cable. 3 dB antennas may also be used on smaller powerboats where the larger 6 dB antenna may be impractical, or long range is not required.

6 dB gain antennas are generally used on powerboats. They achieve greater signal strength to the horizon by limiting their output to 35 degrees above or below horizontal. As power boats do not heel significantly, the reduced vertical radiation angle is not important. 6 dB antennas are typically fibreglass rods about 2.5 m (8 ft) long.

9 dB gain antennas are available, but are rarely used. They are 4 to 7 m (14 to 23 ft) long, and considerably more expensive than 6 db antennas.

What Channels can I Use?

RBR-2 is published here as Appendix 1. It shows all of the assignments of channels for VHF use. The most recent copy of RBR-2 and Radio Aids to Marine Navigation should be consulted to get the most recent information.

In all areas, it is Channel 16 that is to be used for Distress, safety and calling. It is the channel that you may use to make contact with the Coast Guard, although it may be preferable to use a Coast Guard working channel.

If you have DSC, then it is Channel 70 that is used for all DSC calls.

See Appendix 9 and obtain a copy of the latest Radio Aids to Marine Navigation (buy one or download it for free). To determine the working channels or Continous Marine Broadcast channels used by a Coast Guard station, look up that station in section 2 of the book. The book also lists the channels used by bridges, locks and canals.

To determine what channel to use for communication with other boats, look at RBR-2 (appendix 1). Find 'IS' in column IV, (Nature of Service). There must be an 'X' in column III (Area of Operation) for your area. If there is no restriction in Column V that applies to your area, you may use that channel.

Maritime
Radio Course
Student's Notes

Glossary

AIS: **A**utomatic **I**dentification **S**ystem

alarm: In radiotelephone, the signal transmitted to alert Stations that a Distress call and message are to follow.

All Stations: Used to alert all Radio Stations that a message is to follow.

band: A group of radio frequencies designated to a particular radio service.

call: The method used to establish contact with one or more Stations.

call sign: A vessel identifier issued with the station licence by Industry Canada.

CCG: The abbreviation of the **C**anadian **C**oast **G**uard.

CCGA: The abbreviation for **C**anadian **C**oast **G**uard **A**uxiliary.

CCGR: The abbreviation for **C**anadian **C**oast **G**uard **R**adio.

CG: The abbreviation for **C**oast **G**uard.

CPS: The abbreviation for **C**anadian **P**ower & **S**ail **S**quadrons.

certificate: A document showing proof of certification.

channel: A radio frequency that has been designated for a particular purpose.

Class A: A DSC radio specification standard that meets all IMO mf/vhf requirements for compulsorily fitted vessels over 300 GRT.

Class B: A DSC radio specification standard that meets IMO mf/vhf requirements for non-pleasure craft not required to have Class A equipment.

Class C: A DSC radio specification standard that is no longer approved.

Class D: A DSC radio specification standard that meets the minimum vhf/dsc requirements on non-pleasure craft not required to carry Class A or B equipment.(Not all Class D radios meet IMO requirements)

coast station: A shore-based radio station operated by Coast Guard, RCC, etc.

communication: The means of exchanging messages.

compulsory: That which is required by law.

control: To command or direct communications, effected by the Controlling Station.

COSPAS-SARSAT: an orbiting satellite system that detects EPIRB distress signals.

dinghy: A small auxiliary vessel carried or towed by the main vessel.

direction finder: A type of electronic equipment used to obtain bearings from radio signals.

Distress communication: The type of communication used when a station is in 'grave and imminent danger' and requires 'immediate assistance'. The Distress traffic that follows the Distress signal.

DSC: **D**igital **S**elective **C**alling.

duplex: Use of two different frequencies, one for transmitting and the other for receiving.

EPIRB: **E**mergency **P**osition **I**ndicating **R**adio **B**eacon

ETA: **E**stimated **T**ime of **A**rrival

frequency: The number of Hertzian waves per second of an alternating current; radio frequency or channel used for communication.

FRS: **F**amily **R**adio **S**ervice, very short range radios (approximately 2 km).

GMDSS: **G**lobal **M**aritime **D**istress and **S**afety **S**ystem.

GMRS: **G**eneral **M**obile **R**adio **S**ervice

GPS: **G**lobal **P**ositioning **S**ystem using satellites to determine position.

Greenwich Mean Time (GMT): Also known as Coordinated Universal Time (UTC), normally used in all radio telecommunications. The letter "Z" is an accepted abbreviation.

GRS: **G**eneral **R**adio **S**ervice, commonly known as Citizen's Band radios.

GRT: **G**ross **R**egistered **T**ons

HF: **H**igh **F**requency radio; from 3 MHz to 30 MHz.

IMO: **I**nternational **M**aritime **O**rganization

INMARSAT: **I**nternational **M**aritime **Sat**ellite Organization.

intership: The communications link between two ship stations.

ITU: The International Telecommunication Union. The international organization established to provide standardized communication procedures and practices, frequency allocations and radio regulations.

kHz: kilohertz (1000 Hertz).

licences: A document that, unless exempted, radio stations in Canada must obtain. It specifies the call sign assigned to the station, the authorized frequencies, type of radio equipment authorized and any special conditions under which the station should be operated.

LORAN: **Lo**ng **Ra**nge **N**avigation system. Now decomissioned.

Maritime Mobile Service: The radio telecommunications service used by all vessels internationally.

Mayday: The signal used to signify a Distress situation is in effect.

Mayday Relay: The signal used by a station to relay a Distress call and message from the Station in Distress.

MF: **M**edium **F**requency (300 KHz – 3000 KHz)

MF-DSC: **M**edium **F**requency **D**igital **S**elective **C**alling.

MHz: **M**egahertz (1000 KHz).

microphone: The apparatus affixed to the radio which converts sound waves to electrical impulses.

MMSI: **M**aritime **M**obile **S**ervice **I**dentity.

NAVTEX receiver: A radio receiver operating on 518 KHz designed to receive marine safety information, navigation and weather warnings, and SAR alerts.

nm: **n**autical **m**ile.

NOAA: **N**ational **O**ceanic and **A**tmospheric **A**dminstration.

Pan Pan: The signal used to signify an Urgency Situation and that the Station is about to transmit a message concerning the 'safety of a vessel, aircraft, or vehicle or the safety of a person'.

phonetic alphabet: The international method of word spelling to be used when communications may be difficult.

position: The location of the vessel with reference to land positions, aids to navigation, etc.

priority: The order in which radiocommunications may proceed.

procedures: The order and the precise method of conducting radio communications according to ITU regulations.

profane language: Language which is offensive and blasphemous.

radar: A device for finding range and direction by ultra-high radio frequencies which reflect back to their source and display the position and nature of the reflected object.

radio operator: The person certified and authorized to transmit and receive radio communications.

radio silence: While a Distress situation is in progress, all stations must maintain radio silence, unless they are involved in Distress traffic.

radiotelephone (radio): A type of electronic equipment that transmits and receives the radio waves involved in radio voice communications.

RCC: **R**escue **C**oordination **C**entre

ROC(M): **R**estricted **O**perator's **C**ertificate (**M**aritime).

RSS: **R**adio **S**tandards **S**pecification

Safety communications: The transmission of messages dealing with hazards to navigation and meteorological information.

SAR: **S**earch and **R**escue.

SART: **S**earch **a**nd **R**escue **T**ransponder.

SC-101: A discontinued DSC radio specification standard.

sea area: An area within which radio contact with a shore station is possible and areas used by GMDSS to define communication equipment requirements for vessels

sécurité: The signal used to indicate that a Safety message is to follow.

Seelonce: The international word for Silence.

shift: Used to indicate a change to another vhf channel.

ship-to-shore: The communication link between a ship station and a shore station.

ship station: A licensed mobile station.

signal: The transmission of a designated international word or electronic tone that alerts stations that a specific call and/or message are to follow, as it pertains to radio operation.

SSB: **S**ingle **S**ide **B**and

simplex: Use of a single frequency for both transmitting and receiving.

SOLAS: International Convention for **S**afety **o**f **L**ife **a**t **S**ea.

Spectrum Management: The Industry Canada Department responsible for regulating and licensing radio frequencies.

station licence: A licence issued by Industry Canada to vessels not exempt.

summary conviction: When found guilty by a court of law under the Summary Convictions Act.

superfluous communications: Excessive and/or unnecessary communications.

switch to: A request to change to a specific channel.

switch and answer: A request to change to a specific channel and respond to the call.

traffic: Communications between stations.

transceiver: a radio receiver and transmitter combined into a single unit.

transmit: The issuance of radio waves used in communication.

transmit switch: The device attached to the microphone that, when depressed, allows the operator to transmit radio waves.

transponder: A radio transceiver that automatically responds to a radar signal.

Urgency communications: The traffic that follows the Urgency signal 'Pan Pan'.

VHF: Very High Frequency (30 MHz – 300 MHz)

VHF-DSC: Very High Frequency Digital Selective Calling.

voluntary: Optional

VTS: Vessel Traffic System

WWNWS: World Wide Navigational Warning System